Comme je passais à grands pas sous les palmiers, j'entendis quelque chose de semblable à des gémissements.

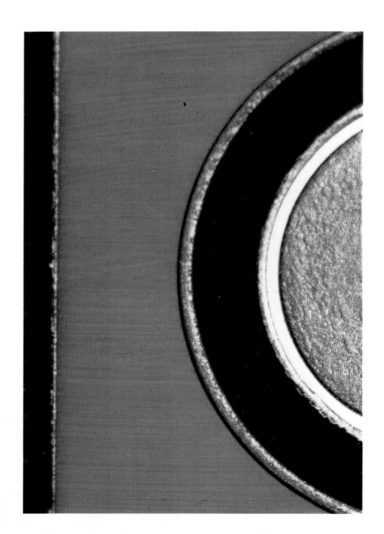

Illustrations on preceding pages:

1   E. G. BENITO, Vanity Fair *magazine cover, June 1924, U.S.A. (Library of Congress, Washington, D.C.,*
Swann Collection)

2   CHARLES LOUPOT, *"St. Raphaël Quinquina," poster, 1938, France (coll. Susan J. Pack)*

3   F.-L. SCHMIED, Daphné *by Alfred de Vigny, book illustration, 1924, France (Leonard Fox Rare Books,*
New York)

4   ANONYMOUS, *untitled, small alamanac cover, 1931, France (coll.*
Sacha Leroy, Bibliothèque Forney, Paris)

5   SYLVAIN SAUVAGE, *untitled, watercolor, c. 1925, France (Jadis et Naguère, Paris)*

PATRICIA FRANTZ KERY

Art Deco Graphics

160201

Thames & Hudson

To Jacques Mallet

ACKNOWLEDGMENTS

It would have been impossible to complete a book such as this without the encouragement, enthusiasm, and generosity of the many people and institutions in a dozen countries who shared with me their precious time and knowledge.

Of these, the following were particularly helpful: Arethon Gallery, Astrid Asseo-Gotsch, Nicholas Bailly, Dr. Ingeborg Becker, Cora H. van de Beek, Marylene Bellenger, Mr. and Mrs. Pierre Bellenger, Merrill C. Berman, Aldis Brown, Robert Brown, Adrian Cochran, Roger Coisman, Delorenzo Gallery, Jacques DeWindt, Martin Diamond, Gilles Didier, Aiden Donovan, Norbert Drey, Bernd Dürr, Terry Eckter, Dr. Lee Ehrenworth, Peter Findlay, Bibliothèque Forney, Leonard Fox, Audrey Friedman, Barry Friedman, Paolo Garretto, Stephen Greengard, Marie-Catherine Grichois, Galerie Grillon, Walter Haas, Felix Hartung, Iris Hoffman, Brigitte Homburg, Margaret Kaplan, Leon Khatchikian, Geneviève LaCambre, Eric Layton, Deborah Glusker Lebrave, Francine Legrand-Kapferer, Anne-Claude Lelieur, Annabel Levitt, Ract Madeux, Haim Manishevitz, Tara McCoy, Susan J. Pack, Dr. Erika Patka, Anne Pfeffer Gallery, France Pier, Dr. Klaus Popitz, Walt and Roger Reed, Susan Reinhold, Jack Rennert, Claudie Roger, Jennifer Roth, Claudia von Schilling, Terry Shargel, Charles Spencer, Mme. Vallois, John Vloemans, Phillip Williams, and Christophe Zagrodski.

I would like to thank three others who were especially supportive. First, Jacques Mallet, who was ever present and indispensable, with artistic, editorial, and emotional support. Jamie Schler and Louise Stoltz were expert researchers who helped enormously with gathering and organizing information.

P.K.

First published in the United Kingdom in 1986 by
Thames & Hudson Ltd, 181A High Holborn, London WC1V 7QX

First paperback printing 2002

Published in the United States of America in paperback in 2002 by
Thames & Hudson Inc., 500 Fifth Avenue, New York, New York 10110

© 1986 Balance House, Ltd.

British Library Cataloguing-in-Publication Data
A catalogue record for this book is available from the British Library

Library of Congress Catalog Card Number: 2001096302

ISBN 0-500-28353-2

Printed and bound in Italy

CONTENTS

EL LISSITZKY, **Wendingen** *magazine cover, 1922, no. 11, The Netherlands (Pat Kery/Jacques Mallet Fine Arts, New York)*

NOTE: In the text, an asterisk (*) after a name or word indicates that there is a relevant illustration in the book. A number in the margin, to the left of the line with the asterisk, gives the page on which the illustration appears.

If an asterisk refers to more than one illustration, the page numbers are given with a comma between. If more than one asterisk appears on any line, the page numbers in the margin are given in the same order, separated by a slash (/).

ILLUSTRATIONS

MAGAZINES

COMMERCIAL DESIGN

BOOKS

FASHION & COSTUME

14

PART 1

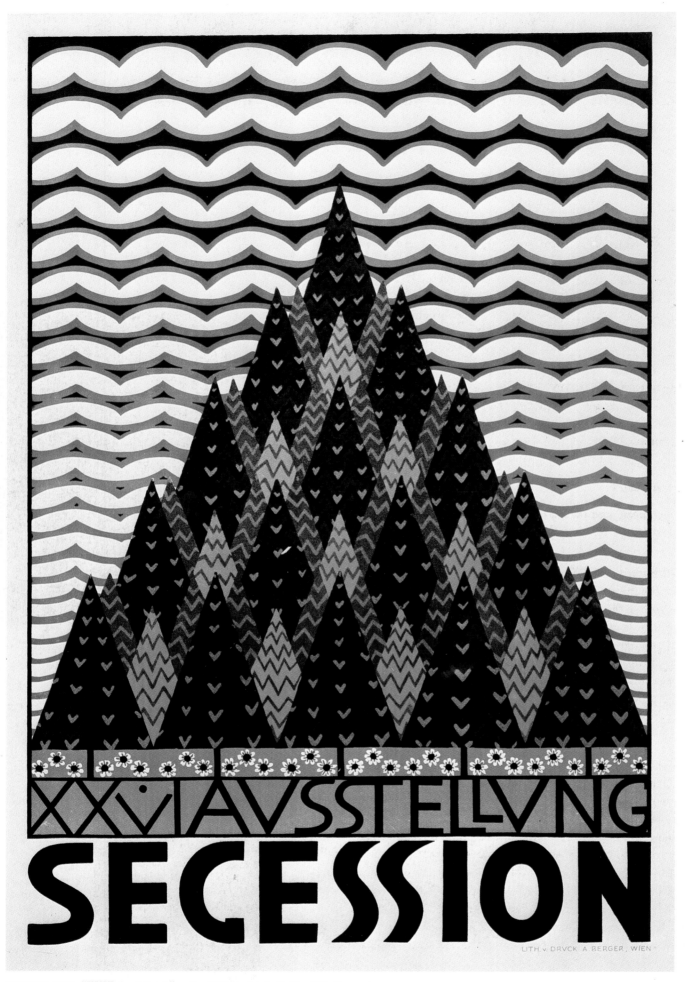

FERDINAND ANDRI, *"XXVI Ausstellung," poster, 1906, Austria (coll. Merrill C. Berman)*

Foundations of
of Art Deco graphic style

Europe entered the twentieth century with a thirst for modernity and liberalism as it broke free of centuries of traditional standards and conventions. Its mood was inspired by the machine and the rapidly expanding technological advancement it represented. Although some, such as Franz Kafka, feared the dehumanizing potential of the machine, its significance for society was a reality that could no longer be denied. Scientific and engineering inventions were not now remote events; they had a powerful impact on people's daily lives. About 1890 Louis H. Sullivan and the Chicago School pioneered the skyscraper; then, in barely a decade, came a stunning succession of technological miracles: the automobile in 1893; the first public cinema show in 1895; transatlantic wireless in 1902; and the Wright brothers' first flight in 1903. It was recognition of the enormously accelerated change in society that ignited the desire for modernity.

The role of the artist

> *My god is machinery, and the art of the future will be the expression of the individual artist through the thousand powers of the machine. . . .*
> Frank Lloyd Wright, 1900

Not all the freethinking artists of Wright's generation shared his optimistic idealism. However, for the progressive early-twentieth-century designer, the question was not whether the machine was to be viewed optimistically or pessimistically, but how to deal with it. The time had come to reconcile art and industry: sensuous, colorful, emotional art and cold, hard, impersonal machines. How could these opposing forces coexist in harmony? Avant-garde artists working in the first four decades of the twentieth century responded by developing startling new visual concepts that matched the radical changes of technology and provided a climate of modernity that made a rapprochement possible.

Graphic design, like the avant-garde art movements, responded to the pressures for modernity, for new forms, for a new visual language. Graphic artists created their own radical innovations and imaginative solutions to meet this challenge, assimilating the inventions of the art movements as well as myriad new ideas that erupted from the progressive society. Unlike painting, the graphic arts *had* to look modern and express the dynamism of the new age, because designers for commerce and industry had to provoke people to buy or to do something. So the best graphics of the period reflected what industrial ingenuity brought to society. As skyscrapers provided powerful new perspectives, exciting vistas, and functional forms, as machines created agitation from their pounding and energy from their speed, graphic artists

JOSEPH BINDER, Fortune *magazine cover, December 1937, U.S.A. (priv. coll.)*

"Chrysler Building New York," 1928–30, photograph by William Van Alen

grasped the changes and incorporated them into their designs. While the radical developments in painting were too esoteric and intellectual to be comprehended quickly by the masses, the graphic arts carried the spirit of modernity into the cultural mainstream via books, magazines, posters, and enormous quantities of printed materials in a wide variety of forms.

The Art Deco style

Modernism is one of the many terms used synonymously with Art Deco. Theoretically, it can be applied to any design that demonstrates the designer's intention to take an entirely new approach, free of restrictions imposed by traditional concepts of form, scale, arrangement, or material. In its time, Art Deco style was called many things: Style Chanel and Style Poiret (after those leading fashion designers); Skyscraper Style, Vertical Style, and New York Style; Art Moderne or Modern (the American term of the late twenties and the thirties); Jazz Style; or simply modernism. The style has been named Art Deco only since 1966, when the Musée des Arts Décoratifs of Paris held a retrospective of works designed in the style that had been shown at the 1925 Paris Exposition des Arts Décoratifs et Industriels Modernes (Exposition of Modern Decorative and Industrial Arts). Art Deco is an abbreviation of the title of that landmark exhibition.

As will be discussed more fully later, Art Deco was a highly diverse style that incorporated many varied, even conflicting, ideals. Unlike previous movements in applied art, including Art Nouveau, Art Deco was not conceived or precipitated by independent groups of artists working with common ideals and standards. Rather, it is a convenient term applied to works that were produced over a period of roughly thirty years prior to World War II, and of which the essence and only true common denominator is an intangible: a mood representing what modernity meant to people in the first half of the twentieth century.

Art Deco was an evolving style, which (like most styles) did not start or stop at a particular moment in history. However, for convenience the beginning date could be called 1908; the apogee, 1925; and the final year, 1939, although there are some important examples found outside that span of time. The first half of the era featured artisan decorative arts, mainly European, and centered in Paris. After 1925 the style shifted to a focus on mass-produced industrial arts and quickly spread to the United States. Before 1925 the artisan was revered as much as the machine was after that. Objects, graphics, and fashions were decorated or crafted using painstaking old-world techniques. In furniture and objets d'art the craftsman often controlled and executed the designs. In the graphic arts, illustrations were often reproduced by handcraft processes, such as lithography and pochoir. When attitudes changed and the machine became the dictator of style, designs changed radically: streamlining, simplicity, and functionality prevailed.

There were two distinct tendencies in the Art Deco style before 1925. The first was toward fashion, which began in 1908 with publication of the pivotal book *Robes de Paul Poiret Racontées par Paul Iribe* (*Dresses by Paul Poiret Presented by Paul Iribe*). In that book there was a totally new look in the dress designs as well as in the illustrations depicting them. Fashions were loose-fitting and provocative; illustrations were simplified, with little detail. In the drawings, reality was transformed; that is, the images reflected not the

GEORGES LEPAPE, Vogue *magazine cover, February 1922, U.S.A.* *(priv. coll.)*

actual world, but one of fantasy. Women's bodies were depicted not with their normal curves and proportions, but rather tubular and slightly elongated. These illustrations of 1908 fully meet the criteria for Art Deco graphic style that are proposed later in this text.

In 1909, the fashion tendency of Art Deco was fortified by the arrival in Paris of Serge Diaghilev's Ballets Russes. This remarkable company ignited a latent passion for visual opulence and sensuality that infused fashion design with these qualities at the same time as it acknowledged the quest for modernity. The sources of inspiration for the latter were the new ideals of simplification, geometricism, elongation, and functionality found in the teachings of the Vienna Secession, the Glasgow School, and various small European workshops, and in the work of progressive architect-designers. Examples of the modern graphic style were seen primarily in French and American magazines before 1925.

The second tendency of the Art Deco style grew out of the avant-garde art movements. Although these movements began to develop just after the turn of the century, they did not have an appreciable effect on the style of graphics until after World War I. When the art-movement tendency developed, it did not replace the other. Rather, it gave substance and strength to what was a somewhat frivolous, unstructured, nonintellectual approach to the style. The art movements inspired several important aspects of Art Deco graphic style: a more radical use of geometricism; tension and agitation from the juxtaposition of forms and fragmentation of images; abstraction; rationalization; extreme simplification. In addition, the Deco graphic designers were inspired by the idealism and intensity of the avant-garde artists.

The scope of this book

This is the first book to focus exclusively on Art Deco graphics. The text discusses in depth the origins, sources, and influences that formed Art Deco graphic style and then covers the many areas of graphic design in which the style appeared. The illustrations shown are basically two-dimensional works made for production in print—posters, magazine covers and illustrations, book jackets and pages, fashion drawings, advertisements, postcards, sheet music covers, menus, packaging, labels, letterheads, textiles, wallpapers, stationery, catalogues and brochures, etc. While the bulk of the book shows these printed works, there is a chapter ("Transition") on decorative paintings and prints that formed a bridge between the fine arts and commercial graphics during the Art Deco period. Throughout the text, marginal illustrations are used to demonstrate relationships and influences in an effort to clarify the nature of Art Deco graphic style—which is the purpose of this book.

GEORGES BRAQUE, House at L'Éstaque, *oil on canvas, 28¾×23½",* *1908 (Kunstmuseum Bern, gift of Herman and Margrit Rupf-Stiftung)*

What is a work of Art Deco graphics?

Despite the fact that Art Deco style—and even more particularly the graphic style—is a complex amalgam of disparate tendencies, subtly shifting in emphasis and mood as it developed over a period of decades, the selection of works to be included in the book demanded a set of criteria that could fairly be said to apply to all the choices. To a very large extent, the choices initially were made by an instinctive response to the intangible spirit of modernity (in the early-twentieth-century sense) referred to earlier. Finally, however, a reasonably specific list of characteristics had to be devised and committed to writing, however qualified it might be.

In making such a list, a search was made for underlying elements, common denominators that link the many diverse works called examples of Art Deco graphic style. Inevitably, account had to be taken of the periphery of the style—the pieces that represent a transition from an influence or earlier style, or works by important Art Deco artists that are less than typical. These the reader will identify according to his or her own judgment, but they are relatively few. Excepting these, all of the works illustrated can be found to reflect, in varying ways, four criteria that seem to be constant, formative components of essential importance: geometric and linear formality; optical simplicity; distortion or transformation of reality; and period representation.

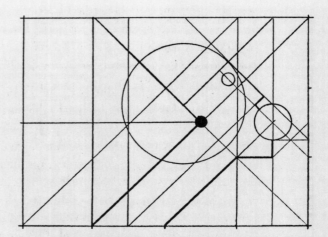

1. GEOMETRIC AND LINEAR FORMALITY

The first tendency of the style, as seen in early fashion illustration, often included geometric elements in the patterns in dresses and pillows, straight-cut hairstyles, slanted or circular eyes, and angled gestures. Linearity was expressed in many ways, such as the drawing of women with tubular bodies and elongated limbs. The second tendency, that derived from the avant-garde, produced designs that might have been conceived with drafting tools in hand, rife with circle, square, and triangle. Geometricism often manifested itself in design composition. (The ultimate example is A.M. Cassandre's
93 diagram showing the underlying structure of his "L'Intrans"* poster.) It is also seen in cubistic montages, certain juxtapositions of design elements, Constructivist linear tensions, and, of great importance, the use of geometrically designed, mechanical-looking, sans-serif type.

A. M. CASSANDRE, *design diagram for poster "L'Intrans," c. 1925, France*

2. OPTICAL SIMPLICITY

In both tendencies of the style there was a move to streamline subjects and design elements, to take them down to their essential features. Reduction was key; less was more. Eyes became two dots; a mouth, a single line. Background detail was reduced or omitted. Ornament was brought under control; if used at all, it was as a significant element of design, rather than randomly to fill space. Indeed, white space was consciously used as an important part of the design. The use of symbols and abstract designs to convey complex visual messages simply and quickly was an aspect of this effort.

E. MCKNIGHT-KAUFFER, *"BP Ethyl Controls Horse Power," poster, 1936, Great Britain*

3. DISTORTION OR TRANSFORMATION OF REALITY

This is a fundamental but seldom noted aspect of Art Deco graphic style. Deco graphic works did not *depict* the real world; they suggested and interpreted it. In the fashion tendency, this was often manifested in the indication of a lifestyle or attitude, such as elegance, refinement, sophistication, optimism. Actually, the Art Deco period was generally a time of turmoil and trouble. The often giddy or elegant face of Art Deco graphics represented desire rather than reality, much like the Hollywood musical extravaganzas of the 1930s. In the second, avant-garde tendency, the distortion of perspective and proportion often occurs—as in Cassandre's poster "L'Atlantique," showing a tall, stately ocean liner next to a tiny tugboat. Distortion created illusions of size, speed, power, agitation, pulsation, and dynamism.

A. M. CASSANDRE, *"L'Atlantique," poster, 1931, France (Posters Please, New York)*

4. PERIOD REPRESENTATION

Period representation—which may only hint at an obscure or subtle element of the modernist mode—is an essential ingredient in any progressive style, and especially in Art Deco. The work of Art Deco graphic designers was deliberately or subconsciously intended to promote the spirit of the age; depending upon the date and country of origin, this could have been a futuristic vision, jazz, elegance, the exotic, speed, power, exuberance, liberation, or even war.

History and development of the style

To understand the Art Deco style in graphic art it is necessary to examine the complex historical background from which the style evolved, as well as developments in other areas of modern art, to which Art Deco graphics are closely linked. These include the avant-garde movements of the early-twentieth-century fine arts and the progressive schools of decorative art, such as the Wiener Werkstätte (Vienna Workshops), as well as influences from the performing arts and fashion. The Bauhaus was crucial in bridging and crystallizing the various movements and developments. These are discussed in detail in the following pages.

Art Deco origins in the progressive decorative arts

The origins of modernism in applied art are rooted in a small number of decorative arts movements and workshops established around the turn of the century, including the Glasgow School, Vienna Secession, and the Deutsche Werkbund (German Work Guild). A primary tenet of these groups was that art should be introduced into all things, from objets d'art to ordinary household items. This emphasis on the importance of design was an essential element in the development of the Art Deco style and taste. The attitude was well described by German designer Herbert Bayer, who wrote, "visual enrichment of life becomes a fundamental outlook because aesthetics encompasses all of man's activities and aspirations."[1]

OSKAR SCHLEMMER, *"Das Triadische Ballett," poster, c. 1924, Germany (Bauhaus-Archiv Museum für Gestaltung, Berlin)*

It is from these pioneer beginnings that artists began to control the use of ornament, move toward abstraction, add geometric elements, and elongate and simplify their designs in the decorative arts. The trend toward conscious control of decoration began in the late nineteenth century, as progressive designers—often architects—rejected the sumptuous ornamentation loved by Victorian revivalists in favor of simpler styles. It was a functional, rational approach to the formation of objects and the design of graphics. Of major inspiration to these architect-designers and their followers was the modern skyscraper, just beginning to make its appearance. A tendency to reject ornament along with a simplification and purification of design culminated in the work of Le Corbusier and the Bauhaus artists. Art Deco artists began to adopt geometric motifs, opposing the curvilinear ones of the Art Nouveau style, and incorporated them as part of the structure of their designs, rather than as ornamentation to fill space.

Top
JOOST SCHMIDT, *"Bauhaus Ausstellung," poster, 1923, Germany (Bauhaus-Archiv Museum für Gestaltung, Berlin)*

GUSTAV KLIMT, Portrait of Adele Bloch Bauer, *oil on canvas, 1907 (Österreichisches Museum, Vienna)*

THE GLASGOW FOUR AND THE WIENER WERKSTÄTTE

Glasgow, Scotland, in the late nineteenth century was an unlikely locale for progressive decorative arts, but it was there that the architect Charles Rennie

Mackintosh established a style that is recognized today as having given birth to modern design consciousness. Mackintosh and his small group of collaborators, known as the "Glasgow Four," which included his wife, Margaret MacDonald, began to redefine the look of everyday objects before the turn of the century, and also contributed to the graphic arts through poster design.

The ideals of Mackintosh were shared by the artists of the Vienna Secession and by fellow architect Josef Hoffmann, who was an original member of the Secession in 1897 and one of the founders of the Wiener Werkstätte in 1903, with Koloman Moser. Both Moser and Hoffmann were exponents of the controlled use of ornament in design, incorporating geometric stylization combined with bold, simple, repetitive forms and linear typography.

Many of those early Viennese graphic works are comparable to the Art Deco style of the late 1920s and 1930s. Some creations can be categorized as Art Deco, but they were important primarily as inspirational designs.

ARCHITECTS AND WORKSHOPS IN GERMANY, ENGLAND, AND FRANCE

A number of design workshops were founded in Germany on lines similar to the Viennese movement, including the Deutsche Werkbund, an activity established in Munich in 1907 by architect Hermann Muthesius. The Germans focused their attention on refining the Jugendstil, or northern European Art Nouveau style, and designed simple, inexpensive objects intended for standardized manufacture on an industrial scale, thus fulfilling the vision of Frank Lloyd Wright. By teaching the modernist aesthetic, they freed designers from the restrictions of traditionalism and anticipated the principles of the Bauhaus. Indeed, the Werkbund was dissolved into the Bauhaus when the latter began in 1919.

An influence that cannot be overlooked is the role of the architects who inspired many young graphic artists to move toward simplification and other modernist ideals as early as the late 1890s. In the forefront were Adolf Loos, Le Corbusier, Mies van der Rohe, Walter Gropius, Frank Lloyd Wright, Hoffmann, Peter Behrens, and Robert Mallet-Stevens, some of whom produced Art Deco designs for interiors, objects, and graphics. They were among the most vocal advocates of modernity, and there was much contact between them. For instance, Le Corbusier and Gropius worked in Behrens's Berlin office. Behrens (who also produced graphics—his poster "A.E.G. Metallfadenlampe" [1907] is a proto–Art Deco work) was instrumental in the formation of the Deutsche Werkbund. Gropius became the first director of the Werkbund's successor, the Bauhaus, and Le Corbusier went on to create his own functional architectural style.

96, 158, 171 The architects' call for purity, new forms, and an integration of all the arts led independent artists such as Lucien Bernhard to produce, as early as 1903, progressive, pared-down graphic designs.* Bernhard went on to create many important Art Deco designs for posters, advertising, and typography. He did not wait for the second tendency of the Art Deco style—that springing from the avant-garde art movements—to influence him, but, like many young graphic artists, learned from the architects' call for change.

Among other organizations that shared this ideal of interaction of the arts were the Omega Workshops, founded in England by Roger Fry in 1913, which produced all kinds of decorative art, with an emphasis on textiles and

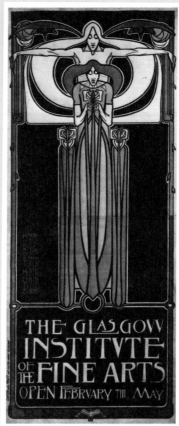

22

HERBERT MCNAIR, MARGARET MACDONALD, AND FRANCES MACDONALD, *"The Glasgow Institute of the Fine Arts," poster, 1896, Scotland (Pat Kery Fine Arts, New York)*

PETER BEHRENS, *"Allgemeine Elektricitäts Gessellschaft," poster, 1907, Germany*

handcraftsmanship. Although their influence on Art Deco graphics was almost nil, the workshops' most important designer, Wyndham Lewis, the founder of Vorticism (an offshoot of Cubism), established several important publications, such as *Blast*,* and had a significant influence on British modernist designers.

In France, the couturier Poiret established his own design workshop and school in 1911, after visiting Hoffmann in Vienna and craft schools in Germany. In the workshop, his Atelier Martine, Poiret assembled a talented group of young designers, including Raoul Dufy. Within only a few years Poiret had become the leading couturier in Paris, inspiring a revolution in women's clothing. With his atelier, he attempted to revitalize all decorative arts by discovering fresh ideas and patterns for use in interior decoration as well as fashion design.

In 1913, Poiret's ateliers in Paris, New York, Berlin, and London were reaping huge profits. However, in the 1920s his elegant style was not consistent with the shift of the Art Deco style toward machine-made modernism, and, shortly after putting on a spectacular show at the 1925 Paris Exposition, he went bankrupt.

The role of the avant-garde

It would be difficult to overestimate the impact of the avant-garde movements on art created in the first quarter of the twentieth century. The unprecedented radicalism of Cubism, Futurism, Dadaism, Constructivism, de Stijl, Fauvism, Expressionism, and other movements shook the art establishment to its roots. It was from these avant-garde movements that geometric patterns, dynamic composition, provocation, and, above all, a new concept of form were added to Art Deco–style designs; a prominent example is the wide adaptation of Modigliani's elongated figures.

FAUVISM, CUBISM, AND LÉGER

The first radical movement was Fauvism, which began around 1900 and influenced the early fashion tendency of the Art Deco style by inspiring a unique use of color. Unlike the other movements, it did not inspire developments in structure and form. As Matisse said, Fauvists were "simply seeking to transpose feelings into color" with the intensity and power of the work of Van Gogh. The movement reached its peak with the Salon des Indépendants of 1906, just when Poiret began changing his fashions by adding new colors and shapes. Fauvism was destined to have an impact on Léon Bakst and Diaghilev, who mounted the Russian Exhibition at the Grand Palais in Paris that year and went on to create their own "orgy of color" three years later with the Ballets Russes, which brought an exotic stimulation to Art Deco.

Of all the modern art movements, Cubism had the most profound influence on the Art Deco style, and Art Deco graphics in particular. Picasso began working on *Les Demoiselles d'Avignon* in 1906. The painting, a pivotal work in the history of modern art, was a complete break from the traditions of the past. Although it was probably not seen by most Art Deco artists, it epitomizes the emotions and ideas that Art Deco artists borrowed from Cubism. Everything about it was disturbing, distorted: primitive heads on the classical nudes, the intense yet vacant staring of the eyes, the angular bodies. In its

AMEDEO MODIGLIANI, Reclining Nude, *oil on canvas, 28½×45⅞",
c. 1919 (coll. The Museum of Modern Art, New York. Mrs. Simon
Guggenheim Fund)*

Top
E. G. BENITO, Vogue *magazine cover, August 13, 1928, U.S.A. (priv.
coll.)*

Bottom
PABLO PICASSO, Les Demoiselles d'Avignon, *oil on canvas, 96×92",
1907 (coll. The Museum of Modern Art, New York. Acquired
through the Lillie P. Bliss Bequest)*

PIERRE THIRIOT, Fleur, *gouache illustration for the revue* L'Arc en
Ciel, *1927 (coll. N. Manonkian, Paris)*

feeling of instability, anonymity, and contrast, it echoed the throbbing vitality of the new urban environment that invaded the serene flow of nature. Taking inspiration from Cézanne, Cubists broke up their subjects into primary forms and showed them from a number of angles at the same time, creating a supreme harmony of the whole. For the graphic artist, these paintings contained exciting new resources for design: geometrical patterns and numerous techniques of fragmentation, montage, and distortion.

Cubist paintings, with their profusion of zigzags, wedges, contrasting squares, and rigid angles, were typical of the works that inspired graphic artists searching for principles of geometrical construction. In Picasso's *Portrait of Ambroise Vollard* (1910), the artist distorted and fragmented his subject. In response, graphic artists gave sharp turns to limbs and body positions, as is evident in Léon Dupin's "Wimereux" (1929) travel poster and in much of the figural work of Paul Colin.

Fernand Léger added to Cubist painting another characteristic that was adopted by the Art Deco designers: the rounded, tubular, statuesque female figure. In his *Three Women* (*Le Grand Déjeuner* [1921]) he accentuated the roundness of the bodies, in contrast to the sharp-edged treatment of Picasso and Braque, and detached whole limbs or body sections to give the figures an automated appearance. Art Deco artists, notably Jean Dupas, often depicted the female form in a manner that can be attributed partly to the influences of Cubism and Léger, and partly to the popularity of the simple, elegant look made fashionable by Coco Chanel.

As the Cubist painters moved further into the realm of abstraction, so did the Art Deco graphic designers. The evolution is clearly visible in Charles Loupot's *Raphaël** advertising series, which spanned more than two decades beginning in the mid-1920s. In a late version of *St. Raphaël Quinquina* he merely silhouetted two waiters in solid colors. One head is a simple ball; the other resembles a chef's hat.*

One of the most important innovations of the Cubists that influenced graphic designers was the use of collage, the application of various materials overlapping on a surface to form a composition of multiple planes. Dynamic designs could be created using existing images (for example, photographs) combined with typography and graphic devices such as bars, lines, or blocks of color. The field of graphic design was no longer limited to individuals with technical skill in illustration or painting; a new wave of designers entered graphics, many from the decorative arts, bringing a variety of talents but sharing the essential ability to conceptualize an idea and then assemble the elements to execute it.

Collage also encouraged the use of symbols, which were essential to the graphic artist as devices to convey an idea or mood quickly. Lightning bolts and whirling wheels symbolized speed and power, a cigarette-smoking woman symbolized her newfound freedom, etc. Picasso expanded the possibilities of collage by including three-dimensional objects in works that were the precursors of the assemblages by Kurt Schwitters and others. The three-dimensional illusion was used as a provocative device in Art Deco graphic art, exemplified by George Bolin's *Vanity Fair* magazine cover of January 1928,* which is built on four overlapping planes. The collage creates energy and stimulates the emotions by disrupting the senses. However, as often happened with cubistic pictures, an overall equilibrium results.

2

168

148

Left
LÉON DUPIN, *"Wimereux Plage,"* poster, 1929, France (coll. Galerie Documents, Paris)

Right
PAUL COLIN, Le Tumulte Noir, *book illustration, 1929, France (Leonard Fox Rare Books, New York)*

Top
PABLO PICASSO, Portrait of Ambroise Vollard, *oil on canvas, 1910 (The Pushkin State Museum of Fine Arts, Moscow)*

Bottom
JEAN DUPAS, *Drawing for Arnold Constable advertisement, 1928, U.S.A. (Gilles Didier, Paris)*

FERNAND LÉGER, Three Women (Le Grand Déjeuner), *oil on canvas, 72¼ × 99", 1921 (coll. The Museum of Modern Art, New York. Mrs. Simon Guggenheim Fund)*

There were a number of important exhibitions of avant-garde art in Paris, London, Munich, and Cologne in the early teens of the twentieth century, but none so far-reaching as the 1913 Armory Show in New York. An outraged public and art critics alike denounced many of the vanguard European paintings as nothing less than barbaric. Almost no one in the United States had seen disjointed images until Marcel Duchamp's *Nude Descending a Staircase* was exhibited there. Duchamp's now famous painting, based on Étienne-Jules Marey's sequential photographs, planted in the minds of graphic artists the idea of suggesting motion through repetition. An example of the repetitive device in Art Deco graphics is "World Dancing Exhibition" a 1926 poster by Hokuu Toda.

Many Cubist paintings, such as Robert Delaunay's *The Red Eiffel Tower* of 1912, exploded with energy and captured the desire of graphic artists to depict the dynamism of a new age. The Eiffel Tower, built for the Paris Exposition Universale of 1889, presented a concrete example of man's dominance over his environment. It was an aesthetically appealing (to some—many Parisians hated it) man-made construction celebrating the conquest of the skies by towering skyscrapers and the airplane, and in turn presented an awesome view from ground level. From the tower's top the public saw the earth as a pattern of geometric grids. These sensational new angles of vision were eventually incorporated into Art Deco graphics to shock and delight the viewer.

ORPHISM AND SIMULTANISM

The artists Robert and Sonia Delaunay, who were linked to Cubism and had considerable influence on Art Deco–style graphics, founded the two avant-garde movements Orphism and Simultanism. Their painting primarily investigated the interaction of large areas of contiguous and contrasting colors, the effects of light on breaking up color space, and the connections between color and movement. Orphism, although short-lived, was the first movement devoted explicitly to nonrepresentational color abstraction. Simultanism regarded color not merely as a decorative adjunct to drawing but as a major element in the creation of form and movement. Sonia Delaunay used the principle of Simultanism in fabric design during the peak years of the Art Deco style, as in the 1926 work shown, and for interiors and fashions.* Creating a trend in colorful geometric patterning, she had her own boutique at the 1925 Paris Exposition to exhibit her fabrics.

292

FUTURISM AND DADA

One aspect of the machine age that was immediately and hungrily absorbed into the Art Deco style was the technology of speed. Futurist artists, intoxicated with speed and space, had a special affection for industrial technology and in particular for the motorcar. Filippo Tommaso Marinetti's Futurist manifesto of 1909 stated, "we affirm that the world's magnificence has been enriched by a new beauty: the beauty of speed." The first Futurist exhibition, held in Paris in 1912, unleashed the visual chaos of the Italian-born movement, its works often including twisting letters and phonetic symbols that formed sounds but made no particular sense. Although painting searched rather unsuccessfully for ways to express the glorious manifesto of the Futurists, Art Deco graphics responded vigorously with dynamic symbols of speed, such as lightning bolts, windswept images, and wheels grinding out

Left
MARCEL DUCHAMP, Nude Descending a Staircase No. 2, *oil on canvas, 58×35", 1912 (Philadelphia Museum of Art, Louise and Walter Arensberg Collection. Copyright ADAGP)*

Right
HOKUU TADA, *"World Dancing Exhibition," poster, 1926, Japan (Museum-Library Musashino Art University, Tokyo)*

ROBERT DELAUNAY, Red Eiffel Tower, *oil on canvas, 49½×35⅜", 1911–12 (Solomon R. Guggenheim Museum, New York)*

Bottom
F. T. MARINETTI, *book cover for Futurist edition of* Poesia, *1914, Italy (from the Mitchell Wolfson Jr. Collection of Decorative and Propaganda Arts, Miami)*

SONIA DELAUNAY, *"Tissu Simultané," textile design, 1926, France (Musée des Arts Décoratifs, Paris)*

power. One of the most important paintings from the movement is *Dynamic Hieroglyphic of the Bal Tabarin* (1912) by Gino Severini, a Cubist-inspired Futurist work that depicts energetic contemporary life rather than the power of the machine, the movement's central theme. The impact of Futurism becomes evident when this work is compared to the Tabarin nightclub poster by Colin.*

GINO SEVERINI, Dynamic Hieroglyphic of the Bal Tabarin, *oil on canvas with sequins, 63⅝×61½", 1912 (coll. The Museum of Modern Art, New York. Acquired through the Lillie P. Bliss Bequest)*

101

Futurism's legacy to the graphic arts is a device more readily identified with the Dada movement: the use of chaotic typography. *Parole in Libertà* (*Words Set Free*) of 1914 attacked traditional concepts in typesetting and layout and presented an entirely new approach to the Art Deco modernists.

Dadaism, according to its "czar," the Romanian poet Tristan Tzara, was a "state of mind," not an art movement. While Futurism was supported by a group of optimists enthusiastic about everything from speed to fashion, Dadaism was a movement of poets, writers, musicians, and artists who were disillusioned with everything from art to war. In an effort to spread its ideals, unify membership, and generate publicity, Dadaists produced numerous publications and presented outrageous, defiant exhibitions (as when an artist read nonsensical poetry with a brioche hanging from one nostril), and planted offshoots of the movement in cities throughout Europe and in New York. Highly visible and provocative, Dadaists encouraged experimentation in all the arts. The movement spread from its inception in Zurich in 1916, at Hugo Ball's Cabaret Voltaire, to Barcelona through Francis Picabia in 1917, to Germany under Max Ernst and Schwitters in 1918, and into Paris with Tzara in 1919. In the United States, Dada was unofficially practiced by Duchamp, Picabia, and Man Ray, who produced unorthodox experiments in art from 1913. Dadaists found their voice in America through *291*, Alfred Stieglitz's publication.

FRANCIS PICABIA, 291 *magazine cover, March 1915, U.S.A. (priv. coll.)*

Bottom
MAX ERNST, The Little Review *magazine cover, 1924, U.S.A. (priv. coll.)*

KURT SCHWITTERS AND THÉO VAN DOESBURG, *"Kleine Dada Soirée," poster, 1923 (Pat Kery Fine Arts, New York)*

Dadaists created pages using an irregular positioning of typography, and developed the use of photomontage, the overlapping and juxtapositioning of photographs, which stimulated Art Deco artists. In the poster by Schwitters and Theo van Doesburg for the "Kleine Dada Soirée" of 1923, the artists used a variety of letter forms and pictorial devices, tipped, twisted, and grouped in what appears to be an arbitrary placement on the page. As with many seemingly random and agitated works in the avant-garde, however, there is a harmony in the design, although it cannot be said that most Dadaist works were harmonious. With his Dada publication *Merz*, Schwitters was at the forefront of this concept of design in his unique page layouts and equally progressive use of assemblage and collage. Standing typography on its head, Ernst used letter forms as an exercise in Dadaism on his cover for the *Little Review*, spelling the most important word, "Review," as ER V/I WE and the word "Winter" with six different letter forms. The Dadaists who experimented with photomontage included the German John Heartfield and the Austrian Raoul Hausmann, who were to inspire numerous Art Deco artists. The technique was used to dramatic effect by Russian cinema posterists in the late 1920s, and was the favorite tool of Swiss artist and photographer Herbert Matter, who designed a number of photomontage travel posters in the 1930s, such as "All Roads Lead to Switzerland."*

71

ABSTRACTION AND EXPRESSIONISM

One of the most influential figures in the fine and graphic arts during the early development of the Art Deco style was the Russian painter Wassily

Kandinsky. From his early work in the Blaue Reiter (Blue Rider) group to his teaching at the Bauhaus and his independent development of abstraction, Kandinsky was a pioneer for the entire art community. He began rejecting perspective and abandoning representation in his paintings around 1910, and came to consider his canvas as a complete sphere rather than a linear plane. While the Constructivists, Cubists, and Bauhaus group all strove for structure and logic, Kandinsky at first favored the intuitive approach of the German Expressionists. By the early twenties he had turned to pure abstraction. Art Deco graphic and decorative artists were especially influenced by his abstract paintings, which were reflected in much of their work, as can be 196 seen in the French stationery design shown.* His influence was particularly important on wallpaper and textile designs produced at the Bauhaus.

The German style of Expressionism from 1914 to 1924 had less effect on the content of Art Deco graphics and more on the concept of provocation through the distortion of images. Its basic outlook of pessimism and disgust at the injustices of the world was contrary to the optimism expressed by the followers of Art Deco, and the ideals of the movement were unable to penetrate the Art Deco modernist consciousness. The influence of Expressionism was in the energy of its generally discordant style, rather than in its individual works. The highly charged emotion of Expressionism is unmistakably present in Walter Kampmann's title page for the German magazine *Das* 154 *Plakat** (1921), conceived at the height of the movement.

CONSTRUCTIVISM, SURREALISM, AND DE STIJL

Cubism was instrumental in giving Art Deco graphics their geometric patterns and designs; Constructivism was the movement that taught structure and composition. Constructivist ideals stressed logic and organization, essential elements needed for the emerging graphic artists to be effective in a commercial modern age. Many dynamic compositions of the Art Deco graphic style relied on the innovations of the Constructivists, including certain uses of multiple planes and tipped axes. The principal sources of these concepts were the pioneering work of three Russians: Kasimir Malevich and Vladimir Tatlin, who preferred bold black-and-white forms, and the prolific El Lissitzky, who explored the provocative quality of tension in Constructivist design and disseminated his ideas throughout Europe, establishing publi- 154 cations* for this purpose in several countries. Other Constructivists, such as 207 Alexander Rodchenko, his wife Varvara Stepanova,* Liubov Popova, and 136 Alexandra Exter, together with Rayonists Mikhail Larionov* and Natalia 55 Goncharova,* made important contributions to the Art Deco commercial style in their designs for posters, textiles, theatrical sets, costumes, books, and magazine covers.

Surrealism, rooted in Dada and founded from the remnants of that movement, did not take hold until the mid-twenties peak of the Art Deco style. It had little effect on graphics in comparison to other schools, with symbolism being the only discernible influence.

The Dutch de Stijl movement, founded in 1917 and evident primarily in the work of Piet Mondrian, Bart van der Leck, and Van Doesburg, was concerned with the harmony of color and the Constructivist-inspired concepts of asymmetrical balance and tension in visual forms. De Stijl artists developed a sophisticated, harmonious style that corresponded with the principles of modernism. Their significance was not only in the balanced geometry they

WASSILY KANDINSKY, Cross Stroke, *oil on canvas, 55¼×79", 1923 (Kunstsammlung Nord-Rhein, Westfalen, Dusseldorf)*

27

ÉDOUARD BENEDICTUS, Projet de Boîtes Laquées, *c. 1925, France (Jadis et Naguère, Paris)*

Below right
ANONYMOUS, *graphic design*, Der Sturm, *c. 1915, Germany (Hartung & Karl, Munich)*

ERICH HECKEL, "Kaiser Wilhelm Museum," *poster, 1920, Germany (Jacques Mallet Fine Arts, New York)*

FERNAND LÉGER, "L'Inhumaine," *poster, 1924, France (priv. coll.)*

created and the introduction of bars and grids into graphic layout, but also in their dedication to simplicity and the elegance that accompanied it.

The Bauhaus and progressive graphic design

The Bauhaus group, influenced by Constructivism, de Stijl, and other movements, was the single most important influence on progressive graphic design after its establishment at Weimar in 1919. However, despite the presence of Kandinsky, no important developments grew from the Bauhaus printing workshops until 1923,* when László Moholy-Nagy joined the teaching faculty. Under Moholy-Nagy students were taught to consider the structural aspects of graphics. He stressed "workable" principles of art, emphasizing standardization, simplicity, and rationality as primary objectives. Moholy-Nagy's "dynamic, eccentric equilibrium" was the central concept in a graphic technique based on asymmetrical layouts and an emphasis on the use of white space.

21, 159

The creation of the Bauhaus and the unfolding of its ideology coincided with the period of maximum popularity of the Art Deco style, but the school's influence reached far beyond the decorative arts of the 1920s, as Bayer, Moholy-Nagy's disciple, pointed out in 1967 in his autobiography[2]: "The Bauhaus movement cannot be seen as historically terminated and immutably fulfilled. It changed the world of art, design, and architecture and continues, when its principles are observed, to be a creative force."

Typography in Art Deco graphic style

Lettering, which generally means type, is a major element in almost all Art Deco graphic work, and it is justifiable to examine the development of typography as a separate element in the Art Deco style.

Typography is concerned with both the design and the arrangement of type (which was metal type throughout the Art Deco era). Both aspects were strongly affected by the tendencies of the time, and both acquired characteristics that became typical of Art Deco graphic style.

The reductionist, functionalist tendencies of Deco design were served by the promotion of sans-serif faces by the Constructivists and, most particularly, by the Bauhaus. These serifless types were first produced in 1832 and were used for posters and promotional materials through most of the nineteenth century, but on a limited basis. When the movement toward simple, mechanical-looking design developed at the end of World War I, the sans-serif faces—called "grotesques" in England and "gothics" in America (neither term being very complimentary)—were revived.

Several alphabets were designed at the time with the object of creating a type that would be consistent with the aesthetics of the machine-age ideal of standardization and would be universal in application. Edward Johnston produced one such alphabet for the London Underground Railways posters in 1916, before the Bauhaus experimentation. Both Jan Tschichold and Bayer designed experimental alphabets in Germany in the 1920s, featuring letters formed with ruled lines and the arcs of circles, and no capitals. Bayer's was used for Bauhaus publications for several years beginning in 1925.

The introduction of a serifless alphabet without capitals for general use had

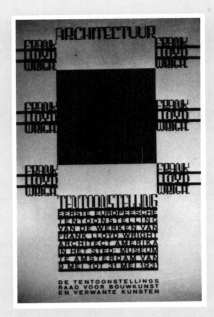

28

H. T. WYDEVELD, "Frank Lloyd Wright exhibition," poster, 1931, The Netherlands (John Vloemans Antiquarian Books, The Hague)

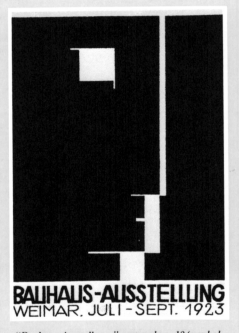

HERBERT BAYER, "Bauhaus Ausstellung," postcard no. 12 (symbol designed by Oskar Schlemmer), 1923, Germany (Bauhaus-Archiv Museum für Gestaltung, Berlin)

für den neuen mens
nur das gleichgewic
natur und geist zu
punkt der vergange

JAN TSCHICHOLD, experimental alphabet, 1929, Germany

BIFUR

special significance as a reform in Germany, where capitals are used for all nouns and much of the printing was in the complicated fraktur, or blackletter (also, confusingly, called "gothic" in America), style of type.

Many designers made contributions to the development of the new typography, most notably Tschichold, who was the doyen of the radical typographers in the 1920s and early 1930s. His *Die Neue Typographie*, published in Berlin in 1928, became the manifesto and the bible of the movement. In the page "Qu'est-ce que la Nouvelle Typographie" he created startling new graphic combinations by manipulating the weight and position of the letter forms in the heading. Piet Zwart's page "Hot Spots" (1930) demonstrated an energetic, communicative design, modern in its purity and spareness of conception, in its use of white space, and in the eccentric but subtle balance of its elements.

As Art Deco typographic style developed from the functional and the starkly modern toward a less severe, lighter, and more elegant mode, the sans-serif typefaces were modified. No longer of uniform or nearly uniform thickness with geometrically formed characters, they began to feature contrasts between thick and thin lines and design idiosyncrasies. The idea of omitting capitals was dropped so far as text was concerned, but survived in the treatment of headlines.

The archetypal Art Deco typeface as we perceive it today is M. F. Benton's Broadway, a high-contrast design produced in 1929 by ATF. During the 1920s there were many variants of the "modified sans," such as Rudolf Koch's Neuland (1923), J. Erbar's Feder Italic (1924), Benton's Parisian (1928), and Cassandre's Bifur (1929). At the same time, and well into the 1930s, several sans-serifs closer to the "universal" models were produced, including Erbar's Erbar (1922), Koch's Kabel (1927), Paul Renner's Futura (1928), Eric Gill's Gill Sans (1928), W. A. Dwiggins's Metro (1929), and a number of faces issued without design credit by typefounders, such as Stephenson Blake's Vogue (1929) and Granby (1930), Amsterdam's Nobel (1929), and Nebiolo's Semplicità (1931). All of these faces were issued with variations of weight and width. Most of them were used extensively in Art Deco graphics. When the contrasting-weight sans-serifs became popular, artists brought back into use the high-contrast Bodonis (Ultra-Bodoni, Engraver's Bodoni, etc.) and their variants.

The rigid limitations of metal-type composition were generally unavoidable in book and magazine design. For posters and some advertising uses designers were able to use hand lettering and achieve more personal alphabets. This was particularly true for posters, which were usually printed by lithography, where no additional cost was involved in the use of lettering. Nevertheless, the lettering styles used on Deco posters tended to follow the designs of the prevalent typefaces.

The arrangement of type for Art Deco graphics was inhibited by the necessities of metal-type composition and letterpress printing even more than was the choice of letter designs. Where Deco layout tended toward the use of diagonals and a generally eccentric spatial organization, letterpress technology was wedded to rectangular units locked into a rectangular frame (the chase) parallel to the page's edge. It is possible to set lines on angles and even curves with metal type, but it is expensive and time-consuming. For mass-produced printing such expenditures were generally avoided. As a result, in

29

JAN TSCHICHOLD, *"Qu'est-ce que La Nouvelle Typographie,"* Arts et Métiers Graphiques *magazine page design, c. 1930, France*

PIET ZWART, *"Hot Spots," advertisement, 1921, The Netherlands*

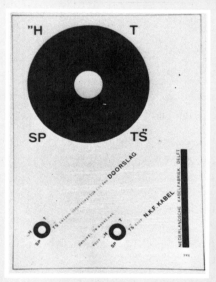

ABCDEFGHJ
Broadway

ART DECO GR
Moderne
Parisian

Below: three weights of Gill Sans

ABCDEFGHIJKLMNOP
abcdefghijklmnopqrstuv

ABCDEFGHIJKLMNOP
abcdefghijklmnopqrstuv

ABCDEFGHIJKLMNOPQR
abcdefghijklmnopqrstuv

books and other publications where large amounts of type were to be set, page layouts tended to be traditional, even when the typefaces were not. In posters and advertisements there was much more freedom to employ the dynamic layouts characteristic of Art Deco graphic design.

Art Deco's many influences

The years 1908 to 1925—a time during which the Art Deco style took root in Paris—reflected a unique period in history. Europe was experiencing social, political, and economic upheavals that included the First World War, while Paris became not only the center of the avant-garde movements but the main focus for artistic activity in the Western world.

THE CALL OF THE WILD

Many influences on the Art Deco style were drawn from exotic lands and cultures. Europe's fascination with the Orient had existed for centuries, but the French developed a love affair with the images of Persia and a legendary Orient during the early Art Deco period, prompted by popular romantic literature and the performing arts. The extraordinary talents of Diaghilev and the Ballets Russes brought an Oriental flavor to the Paris stage with their performances of *Cléopatra* in 1909 and *Schéhérazade* in 1910. Gabriel Mourey, the art critic, called the impact of the Ballets Russes on the artistic community of Paris as great as that of the introduction of Japanese art in the third quarter of the nineteenth century.

There was an enormous fascination with black culture which began with Picasso's attention to African masks in the early years of the century and culminated in the Paris Exposition Coloniale in 1931. The full effect of the obsession was not felt, however, until the uninhibited black American singer and dancer Josephine Baker was introduced to the Paris stage in 1925. The "Black Pearl," as Parisians called her, electrified audiences as she danced wearing only a string of bananas and gold-painted fingernails. (She was just as shocking offstage, appearing in public wearing a live snake around her neck and accompanied by her pet leopard, Chiquita.) The ensuing commercialization of the African exotic included the decorative use of animal forms and the popularity of animal hides and snakeskin in interior design.

During the 1920s and 1930s an equally visible impact was made by the images of France's Pacific colonies. These were commonly expressed in Art Deco graphics by stylized tropical flora and fauna,* and were manifest in the decorative arts in the form of Oceanic masks and figures as well as exotic woods. Central and South America also presented a wealth of visually stimulating imagery, including the geometric motifs of Aztec and Mayan art and the complex, semiabstract compositions of the Incan culture, which were readily integrated into the Art Deco style. For graphic artists the Aztec stairsteps were a perfect symbol of the future.

Egyptian influence during the Art Deco period was given impetus with Howard Carter's discovery of Tutankhamen's tomb in 1922. To graphic artists who were just beginning to understand the power of symbols, learned primarily from the vanguard art movements then penetrating society, the pyramid, pointing majestically and geometrically toward the sky, symbolized the future and the contemporary skyscraper. Deco artists often used the

118

W. H. DEFFKE, *"Kaffe-R," trademark*

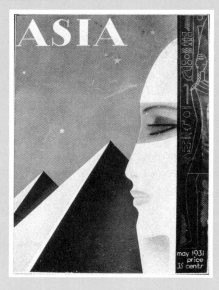

ORSI, *"La Revue Nègre, Théâtre de L'Étoile,"* poster, 1925, France (coll. Museum and Archive, National Institute of Technology, Kyoto)

FRANK MCINTOSH, Asia *magazine cover, May 1931, U.S.A. (priv. coll.)*

pyramid, as well as similar abstract forms it inspired, in a monumental perspective to make it seem even more immense than it actually was.

THE CHANGING ROLE OF WOMEN

Of all the influences on Art Deco, it was perhaps the emerging independence of women that had the most important effect. The effect began to take root with the revolutionary changes in women's fashions, and much of the early development of the style reflected this phenomenon. Poiret sparked the change by freeing women from the whalebone corset, which created a stir not unlike the mini-skirt furor of the 1960s. Women following the avant-garde became adventurous, flirtatious, even brazen with their new emancipation—which was officially confirmed in France, Great Britain, and the United States with laws enacted about 1920. The societal attitudes encircling this (partially) liberated female were central to the Art Deco style. Besides affecting fashions and attitudes in general, the wave of liberalism encouraged physical fitness, sport, and travel. Industry responded by creating luxurious transportation on railways, in automobiles, and on magnificent ocean liners. In the graphic arts a wealth of posters, brochures, postcards, and magazine illustrations depicted and reinforced the trend.

THE 1925 PARIS EXPOSITION

All of the elements that the transient style of Art Deco comprised were displayed and celebrated in Paris in 1925 at the famous Exposition. The Exposition had been planned for 1915 as a stimulus to French designers, but was postponed because of World War I. In the intervening decade, particularly after 1920, Art Deco style developed rapidly, so that what was originally intended as an effort to provoke modernism became a display and celebration of the new style.

COQUEMER, *"Soirée Musicale," invitation, 1925, France (Musée des Arts Décoratifs, Paris)*

It was an elaborate event of unprecedented proportions, including fairgrounds, theaters, and pavilions from French and foreign participants cramming the Grand Palais, with some constructed on barges moored on the Seine, and other impressive structures built by the finest architects of the day. Avant-garde paintings and graphics were widely displayed, including many works by Léger and one of Robert Delaunay's famous Cubist paintings of the Eiffel Tower. Marie Laurencin decorated the French Embassy pavilion. Three posters were commissioned to promote the event, from Robert Bonfils, Girard, and Loupot. Magazine pavilions abounded, including one for *Femina*, with larger pavilions for the influential publications *L'Illustration* and *Arts et Décoration*, both of which were leaders in presenting Art Deco illustration and progressive design.

The exhibition celebrated the luxurious Art Deco style, but, as with all pinnacle achievements, it also heralded the inevitable decline. The progressiveness that was an essential element in modernist design was represented by the stark tubular steel and chrome furniture and industrially designed objects displayed by Le Corbusier and others in the Pavilion de l'Esprit Nouveau. Le Corbusier remarked: "1925 marks the turning point in the quarrel between the old and the new. After 1925, the antique lovers will have virtually ended their lives, and productive industrial effort will be based on the new."

The drive for modernity succeeded, perhaps too well. The advance of industrialism brought with it a withering of the sense of elegance and gaiety that

CHARLES LOUPOT, *"1925 Paris Exposition," poster, 1925, France (Pat Kery Fine Arts, New York)*

marked the early Art Deco era, and the years following the Paris Exposition saw a gradual dissolution of Deco style into other trends—but it was a dissolution with many brilliant interludes.

The Art Deco revival

Art Deco seemed to have died out by 1939, at the beginning of World War II, but apparently its essence was only dormant. The revival of interest in Art Deco sparked by the 1966 Paris commemorative exhibition led to another large show in 1971, at the Minneapolis Institute of Art. A wave of enthusiasm for Art Deco style among important American architects, such as Michael Graves, led to a reprise of the early history of the style, when architects carried progressive architectural and industrial design concepts into the field of graphics. In the early 1970s, a strong Art Deco flavor was introduced into graphic design in the United States by the notable Push Pin Studio, created by Milton Glaser, Seymour Chwast, and others. An Art Nouveau revival began at about the same time, but it was Deco that showed the greater staying power. It is still extremely popular and going strong at this writing.

PART 2

Transition

The late nineteenth century saw a fundamental shift in human experience, caused by the domination of society by industry. The world of man and nature became one of man and culture. Early-twentieth-century artists faced a dual challenge: to question all traditions and conventions and to interpret the world created by industrialization. Artists at every level accepted this challenge, and many of them transformed their art to reflect the new conditions of life.

Progressive painters and sculptors were concerned with creating a new language of art to interpret modern experience and provide a context in which artists could develop their ideas. Graphic designers interpreted and promoted the ideals and modes of daily life in order to enhance commerce. Other artists formed a bridge between the two. Their work is a continuation of the attitudes, forms, and styles developed by the leaders of the avant-garde. This chapter explores that aspect of art in order to show the transition of the Art Deco style from the avant-garde to popular graphics and the diffusion of its various influences.

Some of the artists whose work is shown in this chapter were demonstrably in tune with popular taste. They used the avant-garde vocabulary, but their first priority was style, and their work was meant to please. Others were more serious artists whose work happened to be particularly imbued with the modernist spirit and included the basic features of Art Deco style. Still others were artists of real stature who occasionally did work that qualifies for inclusion here. The works are shown as relevant to the point, but it is for the reader to categorize the artists.

Art Deco painters often seemed preoccupied with representing attractive women. One example is Kees van Dongen, a particularly interesting artist of the period, who did not need to change the nature of his pictures to suit the various purposes of his work. The women he depicted in his commercial work were often exactly like the wide-eyed, long-limbed women in his paintings, and were not unlike those created by the fashion artists. Tamara de Lempicka, who was perhaps the best of all in painting the woman of her times, herself represented the ideal woman of the twenties: she was beautiful, stylish, rich, and famous, and she moved in the best avant-garde circles. *La Belle Rafaela** and *Les Jeunes Filles* are typical of her work. Her figures were plump and rounded, like Léger's, but with a fleshy rather than mechanical appearance. They were always sensuous and alluring, but projected a certain air of fantasy. Often, as in *Les Jeunes Filles*, there was a Manhattan-like street scene in the background.

Dupas,* Jean-Gabriel Domergue,* and Marcel Vertès, all of whom did graphic work in Deco style as well as painting, also focused on the woman of

KEES VAN DONGEN, La Jeune Femme aux Lys, *oil on canvas*, 70⅞×47¼", *c. 1927–29 (courtesy Sotheby's, New York)*

TAMARA DE LEMPICKA, Les Jeunes Filles, *oil on canvas, 1929 (Barry Friedman, New York)*

the day, though not nearly as impressively as Lempicka. Dupas was totally at
51 home with Art Deco stylization, as seen in his painting *Aquarius*.* Over and
over he depicted the same type of elongated, statuesque woman, which to him
represented the ideal beauty of the period. Louis Icart, a very popular French
printmaker, produced more than four hundred drypoints and etchings representing beautiful demoiselles with borzois and other symbols of Art Deco
48 opulence and luxury—but always with a touch of romance and play.* Jean-
Émile Laboureur made prints that straddled Cubism and Art Deco. One of
many artists who adapted Cubism to commercial graphics, Laboureur
combined elongated figures and stylized poses with Cubist geometrics to
260 create images of energy and vitality.*

Although painting in Germany was concerned less with style than with social
and political activism, Alexei Jawlensky—who had joined Klee, Franz Marc,
August Macke, and Kandinsky in the Blue Rider group—produced paintings
and prints featuring what could be considered a very stylized Deco woman,
not unlike those of the fashion artists, particularly Edouard Garcia Benito.
50 In *Sounds of Winter** (1927) Jawlensky created a marvelous face in the cubistic style. Marc and Macke also produced work using flat planes of color and
cubistic sensibilities that strongly reflected the style of the time. Very different, but still revealing aspects of the Art Deco style, are Ernst Ludwig Kirchner's Berlin *Street* paintings of around 1913.

A number of Hungarian artists who regularly exhibited in Berlin between
1913 and 1932 made paintings with their own modernist interpretations of the
44 times. Lajos Kassák, Béla Kádár, Hugo Scheiber,* and Moholy-Nagy were
45 the most notable. Two paintings by Kassák, one an untitled abstraction* and
the other a representational work, *Citroën*, show two very different aspects of
his work that express the flavor of the period.

Some impressive abstract and semiabstract work was produced by Belgian
45 painters, including Floris Jespers, M. L. Baugniet,* Pierre Louis Flouquet,
52 and Victor Servranckx. The figure in Jespers's *Jeune Fille en Mauve*,*
painted on glass, looks not unlike the fashionable elongated women found on
38 the covers of *Vogue* in the period. Baugniet's watercolor *The Kiss** (1925), an
intricate design of circles, relates the couple to the modernist style by elongat-
ing and rounding the man's head and waving the woman's hair, as was often
done in fashion illustration.

Joseph Csaky's watercolors take on an Art Deco appearance with their use of
41 circles, squares, and rectangles. His untitled picture of a mother and child*
incorporates both Cubist and Constructivist elements. Steel girders in the
background allude to the modern fascination with construction.

In Great Britain, Wyndham Lewis prominently represented the modern style
156 in his paintings as well as his graphics.* *Boxing at Juan-les-Pins* was one of
his many efforts to modernize English art. As the founder of Vorticism, Lewis
had a modest but legitimate role in the international avant-garde.

Other European artists whose work had characteristics of Art Deco style
included Archipenko, Michel Goyot, René Herbst, T. L. Mafrazo, Marcous-
50 sis, Dunoyer de Ségonzac, Gleizes, Souza-Cardosa,* Severini, Max Weber,
Lhote, and Jean Lambert-Rucki. Lambert-Rucki's work is particularly interesting, as he specialized in paintings about black jazz. With cubistic geometry
39 he created *Negro Spirituals** in 1921, showing silhouettes of black men and a
guitar against the outline of a modern city skyline. Later, as in his 1935 painting *Kiss*, his work became more abstract.

LAJOS KASSÁK, Citroën, *gouache, c. 1925 (Galerie Opium, Paris)*

In the United States, Arthur Dove, Stuart Davis, Ralston Crawford, Charles Demuth, and Charles Sheeler were among those painting in the modernist style. Dove created his own abstract style, developing his jagged edges and rhythmic contours from nature rather than Cubism. Davis, on the other hand, had lived in Paris for a year around 1928, and his geometric patterning was strongly influenced by Cubist collage. Demuth and Sheeler were more representational, but they treated their subjects in a simplified way, with a Cubist-derived emphasis on geometrical form. Their work often portrayed factories, city buildings, and grain elevators, subjects that emphasized the industrial aspect of modernism. Another group of American artists who painted abstractions in Cubist style worked in New Mexico in the last years of the Deco period. They included Emil Bisttram, Edward Garman, and
37 Raymond Jonson.* Oscar Bluemner's *Jersey Silkmills* (c. 1917) and *Secluded*
42 *Spot—Red Amidst Grey** (1929) also reflect the Cubist interest in factory views and architectural forms.

36

American artists Edward Hopper, Rockwell Kent, Yasuo Kuniyoshi, Louis
43 Lozowick, and Grant Wood* created paintings and prints with much styliza-tion of the period. Lozowick, born in Kiev, formed his style when he met Lissitzky and other Constructivists in Berlin between 1920 and 1924. *Through the Brooklyn Bridge*, his lithograph of 1938, was one of many pictures he made of the bridge, whose beautiful arches and geometric cable strands, symbolizing modern power and grace, fascinated artists of the period.

Although photography was first valued as a way to realistically capture people and places, there were some who came to see it as an art medium.
124 Artist-photographers like Man Ray, Moholy-Nagy, and Edward Steichen* led the experimentation of the twenties. Their work produced a number of nonrealistic photographs with Art Deco characteristics. One of these is Man
46 Ray's *Kiki and the African Mask*,* in which the subject's head is at a right angle to one of the symbols of the era.

LOUIS LOZOWICK, Through the Brooklyn Bridge, *lithograph, 1938, (courtesy Hirschl & Adler Galleries, New York)*

RAYMOND JONSON, **Abstraction in Yellow,** *oil on canvas, 1932 (priv. coll.)*

M. L. BAUGNIET, **The Kiss**, *watercolor, 1925 (Galerie DeWindt, Brussels)*

ÉDOUARD CHIMOT, *untitled, etching, c. 1930 (Pat Kery Fine Arts, New York)*

JEAN LAMBERT-RUCKI, Negro Spirituals, *oil on canvas, 1921 (Bruhan Gallery, Berlin)*

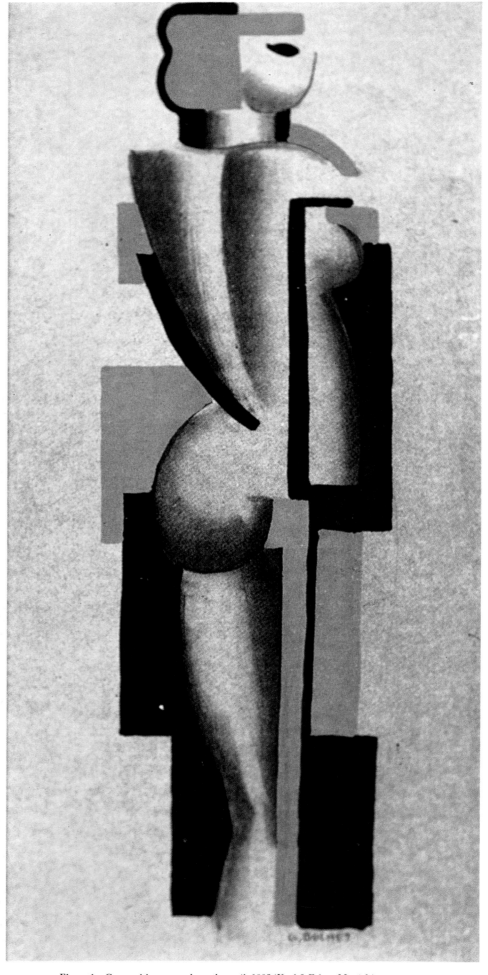

G.-L. BUCHET, Figurative Composition, *gouache and pencil, 1935 (Karl & Faber, Munich)*

JOSEPH CSÁKY, *untitled, watercolor, c. 1930 (Galerie Vallois, Paris)*

MARIE LAURENCIN, Jeunes Filles au Balcon, *etching, 1928 (Pat Kery Fine Arts, New York)*

OSCAR BLUEMNER, Secluded Spot—Red Amidst Grey, *oil on board, 1928–29 (priv. coll.)*

ANDRÉ EVARD, Roses Jaunes, *drawing, 1924 (Karl & Faber, Munich)*

JEAN DUNAND, *untitled, lacquer panel, 1925 (coll. N. Manonkian, Paris)*

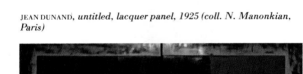

GRANT WOOD, March, *lithograph, 1939 (courtesy Hirschl & Adler Galleries, New York)*

TAMARA DE LEMPICKA, La Belle Rafaela, *oil on canvas, 1927 (courtesy Sotheby's, New York)*

HUGO SCHEIBER, *untitled, gouache and ink on paper, 1922*

M. L. BAUGNIET, Aeroplan Rose Bleu, *oil on canvas, 1926 (Galerie*
Opium, Paris)

LAJOS KASSÁK, *untitled, mixed media, c. 1925 (Galerie Opium, Paris)*

KAREL TEIGE, *untitled, photocollage, c. 1930 (John Vloemans Antiquarian Books, The Hague)*

MAN RAY, **Kiki and the African Mask**, *photograph, 1926 (courtesy Christie's, New York)*

JEAN HANAU, *untitled, oil on canvas, 1933 (Galerie Walter Haas, Zurich)*

LOUIS ICART, Le Cocktail, *drypoint and etching, 1932 (courtesy Mel Karmel, New York)*

LYONEL FEININGER, Villa am Strand, *woodcut, 1920 (Bauhaus-Archiv Museum für Gestaltung, Berlin)*

AUGUSTE HERBIN, Étude pour Motif Hindou, *oil on canvas, 1920* *(Galerie Opium, Paris)*

AMADEU DE SOUZA-CARDOSA, Study of a Head, *pen and ink, 1912 (from the Mitchell Wolfson Jr. Collection of Decorative and Propaganda Arts, Miami)*

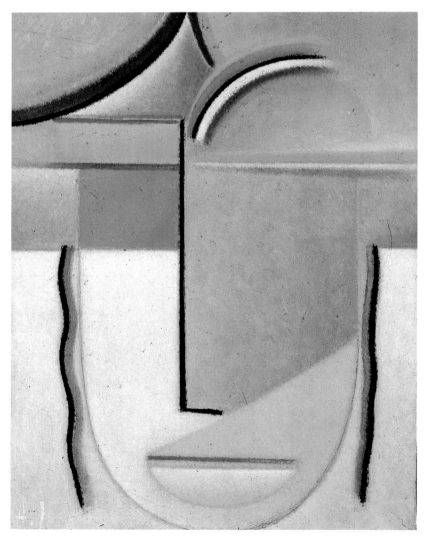

ALEXEI JAWLENSKY, Sounds of Winter, *oil on linen-finish cardboard, 1927 (Norton Simon Museum, The Blue Four Galka Scheyer coll.)*

STUDIO LORELLE, *untitled, photomontage, 1928–29, France (Pat Kery Fine Arts, New York)*

JEAN DUPAS, Aquarius, *oil on canvas, c. 1928 (Primavera Gallery, New York)*

FLORIS JESPERS, **Jeune Fille en Mauve**, *painted on glass, 1928 (Galerie DeWindt, Brussels)*

In the 1890s posters enjoyed a meteoric rise in popularity and evolved into an art form with a language all its own. Three decades later, poster artists in the Art Deco era, inspired by revolutionary art movements, created modern graphics of great vitality and excellent design. Further, they used the ideas of avant-garde art to make posters more effective at their purpose: promoting activities, services, and products. At the moment in history when advertising was trying to become more scientific, posters were in the forefront.

In most of Western Europe, the surge of poster art just before the turn of the century represented an exciting experimental period. New color technology and a renaissance in printmaking enabled artists to make large, colorful images for lithographic printing in quantity. For the first time, artists could expose their work to thousands of people, in the "gallery of the street." Many talented painters, including several who were later recognized as major artists—Toulouse-Lautrec, Villon, Bonnard, Vuillard, Klimt—would try their hand at the medium.

Chéret, Steinlen, Toulouse-Lautrec

In France, the world center of art at the time, the climate for advertising art was agreeable. For example, a French law of 1881 permitted displaying posters on the street. Among the general public, it was not unusual for would-be collectors, excited by the colorful lithographs, to pull them off building walls before the paste had dried. Artists—Alphonse Mucha was one of the most notable—seized the opportunity to print posters in large runs for widespread distribution. In contrast, Viennese officials forbade the sale of small posters to individuals for purposes other than advertising and allowed only licensed lithographers to work directly on the stone. In America, which eventually would lead the world in commercial advertising, posters at the turn of the century were viewed as affordable art for the masses; they cost about ten cents, the price of a popular magazine.

Jules Chéret, in France, pioneered the technique of drawing directly on stone and developed the three-stone lithographic print, enabling artists to control the entire process themselves and to produce multiple full-color prints. Beginning in 1858, Chéret worked for a quarter of a century to perfect the method and popularize posters as a medium, and he is acknowledged as "the father of the poster." He had a major aesthetic and technical influence, producing more than a thousand posters. His exuberant floating figures, typified by stylized red-haired women called "Chérettes," recalled the Romantic period of his youth and its allegorical paintings by artists such as Delacroix, and they lacked the graphic and psychological dynamics of the Art Deco posters.

ANONYMOUS, *Paris street scene with posters, photograph, c. 1931, France (Musée de l'Affiche, Paris)*

Among other early posterists who influenced the poster language of the Art Deco era were Théophile-Alexandre Steinlen, the Beggarstaff Brothers (brothers-in-law James Pryde and William Nicholson), Toulouse-Lautrec, Leonetto Cappiello, Lucien Bernhard, Charles Rennie Mackintosh, and many artists of the Vienna Secession. Rejecting the foliate Art Nouveau look, they anticipated the modern style and developed techniques, like simplification and provocation, for getting a message across in a busy environment. In the Art Deco era there was a dramatic proliferation of advertising messages, which had to compete for the attention of passersby not only with one another but also with the sensory bombardment of speeding vehicles, electric lights, looming skyscrapers, and overhead rapid transit systems. Many of the early artists were influenced by Japanese *Ukiyo-e* prints, which had been "discovered" on the Continent during the nineteenth century. The design of these popular genre illustrations encouraged the use of large, flat areas of color; linearity, with bold, black outlines exaggerating the focal points; and density of composition.

Some artists had moved toward simple imagery, geometric stylization, and abstraction even before the cascade of innovations in art during the early twentieth century. Steinlen's cat posters, "Chat Noir" (1896) and "Lait Pur Stérilisé" (1894), use big swatches of reds and blacks on images of people and animals, often making them appear larger than life. It was in abandoning his sentimental magazine presentation in favor of this powerful poster style that Steinlen emerged as a master. Similarly, the Beggarstaffs reduced poster subjects to their essence, often to silhouettes. Some of their landmark posters were produced by cutting designs in solid-color paper and pasting them on boards or sheets of paper.

The master poster artist of the era was Toulouse-Lautrec. The Beggarstaffs said admiringly of him, "He is one of the few artists who understand what a poster is and should be."[3] Passersby could hardly be indifferent to his dramatic layouts, vibrant colors, and use of contrast. One element in his work that was later used extensively in the Art Deco period was the diagonal, which he borrowed from Japanese prints and from his idol, Degas. Toulouse-Lautrec's usual approach involved an intimate, sideways glance at the subject, with a diagonal device such as a table, a stage, or, in the case of "Jane Avril" (1893), the top of a cello, extending across the poster. Startling perspectives set his forms in motion, as in his first and most famous poster, "Moulin Rouge/LaGoulue" (1891).

BEGGARSTAFF BROTHERS, *"A Trip to Chinatown,"* poster, 1895, Great Britain (priv. coll.)

Cappiello, Bernhard, the Vienna Secession, Mackintosh

After the turn of the century, the frenzied development of poster art all but ceased until the 1920s, except for the efforts of Cappiello. Beginning in 1899 with his instantly successful poster for *Frou Frou* magazine, the Italian dominated French poster art by presenting large, central, and unusual or startling figures: a man breathing fire, for example, or a mischievous green devil. He taught poster artists the value of instant impact with a memorable image.* Cappiello cannot be considered an important Art Deco artist, however, because his style remained his own and he rarely took on the look of the Deco era.

Until World War I it was, in fact, in Germany that the most advanced posters were produced. Bernhard, a Viennese artist living in Germany, along with

87

good info on individual artists

Ludwig Hohlwein, led German poster design for decades before moving to the United States. As early as 1903 Bernhard began to reduce posters to their
158 essentials: product and brand name. His "Priester"* (1903) was considered by Joseph Binder to be a milestone in modern poster design. In this work Bernhard showed only two large matchsticks and a logo. His 1907 "Stiller" poster is equally straightforward. Like many other early graphic designers, Bernhard was intrigued by typography and designed several typefaces, some of which are still in use.

A fascinating early development in poster design was the geometric influence that emanated from Vienna and Glasgow, even before the appearance of the avant-garde movements that are generally credited with that effect. Four early examples from Vienna by Ferdinand Andri, Alfred Roller, Berthold Löffler, and Koloman Moser, all designed between 1902 and 1908, are filled with geometric patterning and stylized elements that would be used extensively by Art Deco artists twenty years later.

16 Andri's "XXVI Ausstellung"* (1904) is the most striking. In it, a geometric pyramid of trees reaches up to the sky, foretelling the next generation's fascination with skyscrapers, and with grandeur in general. It bears an unmis-
17,129 takable resemblance to Joseph Binder's skyscraper cover for *Fortune** magazine, designed over thirty years later in 1937. Binder, an Austrian, spent his formative years designing and teaching in Vienna before moving to the United States. Both Roller's "XIV Ausstellung"* (1902) and Löffler's
108 "Kunstschau Wien"* (1908) show wavy hair on the women, a device used in
107 the coming era of design to depict speed. Moser's "XIII Ausstellung"*
108 (1902) presents three elongated muses with sufficient use of abstraction and geometry that it can be considered a forebear, in spirit, of the next poster era. All of these artists came out of the Vienna Secession, which, although founded in 1897 during the Art Nouveau period, played down or rejected outright the curvilinear excesses of Art Nouveau in favor of geometric forms, functionality, spaciousness, and rationality.

In Glasgow, Mackintosh was working in the same direction. His poster "*The Scottish Musical Review*" (1896) and another, "The Glasgow Institute of
22 Fine Arts"* (also 1896), by the three other artists of his group, the "Glasgow Four," illustrate the conceptual similarities between artists in Glasgow and Vienna: the leaning toward geometricism, linearity, elongation of figures (a device that had a particular impact on fashion illustrations of the early Art Deco period), and repetition. Mackintosh was, in fact, invited to exhibit in Vienna and was honored there more than in his own country.

Cubism, Futurism, Constructivism, and the move toward abstraction

Of all the graphic arts media in the Art Deco period, posters were the one most affected by the art movements that began in the 1900s. In turn, posters carried the spirit of the avant-garde into the cultural mainstream. Cubism, Futurism, Fauvism, Dadaism, Vorticism, de Stijl, and Constructivism were too conceptual and intellectual for the general public, but poster artists used the new principles in their work, which became equally revolutionary.
110 Many important artists riding the crest of the avant-garde—Lissitzky,*
26/27 Goncharova, Schwitters,* Van Doesburg,* Lhote, Kandinsky, Léger,* Utrillo, Foujita, Dufy, and Laurencin—produced at least one poster each.

BERTHOLD LÖFFLER, *"Kunstschau Wien,"* poster, 1908, Austria (Pat Kery Fine Arts, New York)

CHARLES RENNIE MACKINTOSH, *"The Scottish Musical Review,"* poster, 1896, Scotland (coll. Merrill C. Berman)

NATALIA GONCHAROVA, *"Grand Bal de Nuit,"* poster, 1926, France (Musée de l'Affiche, Paris)

Four artists who excelled in applying avant-garde principles to posters were A. M. Cassandre, E. McKnight-Kauffer, Léo Marfurt, and Bernhard. All were expatriates: Cassandre had moved from Russia to Paris; McKnight-Kauffer from the United States to England; Marfurt from Switzerland to Belgium; and Bernhard from Austria to Germany. Each led his adopted country in poster design. "For my part," said McKnight-Kauffer, "the brief research I have made in these movements as a painter has been very beneficial to me in the designing of posters. It has made it possible to make new translations of old forms, it has assisted me in emphasizing the qualities and importance of the use of color and helped to simplify my arrangements of ideas."[4]

Other artists used the radical ideas with varying degrees of comprehension. Some who apparently did not clearly understand the new movements simply used geometric shaping and new techniques to give their posters a superficial look of modernity.

Although all the advanced art movements had some effect on graphic design, Cubism and Futurism were the most important influences initially; the Bauhaus and Constructivism were the most lasting. Posterists adopted a variety of Cubist techniques: an overall geometric presentation, fragmentation of people and objects, overlapping planes, and the combination of real objects and abstraction, to name a few. It was not until World War I, however, nearly a decade after Picasso's early woodcuts of 1907, that Cubism was recognized as a substantial influence. In 1916, *Das Plakat*, the magazine of international poster art, formally recognized the connection when it ran an article about Cubism and posters. But it was not until the mid-1920s that Cubism had its full effect on poster design and the Art Deco style.

116   One of the best examples of a cubistic poster is Bernhard's "Reklame Schau"* of 1929. Bernhard's simple "advertising" style had changed to reflect the style of the period. He divided the face in half, with one side blue, the other orange; made the hands in alternating colors; and further broke up the image by shading the colors in opposite intensities. The face appears plump and sculpted, reminiscent of Léger. The poster was produced for an advertising exhibition in Berlin, where the Bauhaus was breaking new ground with radical concepts of the relationship between art and industry. Indeed, posters in the new manner moved advertising toward the Deco style.

Italian Futurism, with its reverence for speed and power, was another important influence. It gave energy to many poster subjects, not just the airplanes, automobiles, trains, and ships that dominated early-twentieth-century poster art. Founded in 1909, Italian Futurism exalted the power of the machine. "Speed has given us a new notion of space and time," said Gino Severini in his 1913 manifesto, "The Plastic Analogies of Dynamism." The English Futurist manifesto, "Vital English Art," proclaimed: "Forward! HURRAH for motors! HURRAH for speed! HURRAH for draughts! HURRAH for lightning!" Many artists captured the feeling of power in transportation posters, among them Cassandre, Geo Ham, René Vincent, Pierre Louÿs, Alex Kow, and Roger Pérot. Some interpreted the Futurist idea of speed as wind: trees often leaned halfway to the ground, clouds raced in the sky, and hair blew in the wind. Muneji Satomi, a Japanese posterist working in Paris, created this Deco "speeding" effect in his "Japanese Government Railways" poster of 1937. The road and landscape are blurred as if seen from a racing train. Even the telephone poles are dominated by the train's powerful wake.

SERGE GLADKY, *"Jean Borlin,"* poster, c. 1920, France (Deborah Glusker Lebrave, Paris)

SCHULZ-NEUDAMM, *"Metropolis,"* poster, 1926, Germany (priv. coll.)

MUNEJI SATOMI, *"Japan,"* poster, 1937, Japan (Museum-Library Musashino Art University, Tokyo)

Two masterful posters using fragmentation to show speed are Greiwirth's "The Flying Scotsman Again Runs Non-Stop" and Cassandre's "L.M.S.
80 Bestway"* (1928). Both emphasize the cold, steely gray of the train, glorified with a futuristic lightning bolt streaking from the wheels. Cassandre's poster is the more abstract: he showed a close-up of two wheels, the parts that best symbolize power, rather than the traditional full train. He broke up the wheels into a cubistic design of grays, black, and white, with red circles around them to symbolize the heat they generate as they pound the iron
77 tracks. Another locomotive poster by Cassandre, "Nord Express"* (1927), is similar to "L.M.S." in its treatment of speed, but is more brilliant in its total design and typographic style.

GREIWIRTH, *"The Flying Scotsman Again Runs Non-Stop,"* poster, c. 1929, Great Britain (coll. Roger Coisman)

Russian Constructivists and Dutch de Stijl artists completely eliminated realistic objects from their paintings, using pure lines, forms, and colors. Following this development, the first tendency of the posterists was to delete unnecessary details, then exaggerate. Charles Loupot stylized his figures in
2 "St. Raphaël"* (1938) into faceless individuals of unnatural roundness. The tension created by the two plump figures leaning back in their chairs resembles the tension mastered by Constructivists in compositions combining squares, circles, and bars. In the late 1920s, posterists ventured further into abstraction; at times the only thing distinguishing a poster from a fine-art work was a headline or a logo. Phoebus Palast cinema posters in Germany by Jan Tschichold and C. O. Müller also used Constructivist tension, balancing a bar, a circle, and a headline in a modernist composition with de Stijl–influenced colors. Müller's 1927 poster for Phoebus Palast introduces black-and-white photography into the composition. And the poster by H. T. Wydeveld (publisher of the Dutch avant-garde architectural magazine *Wendingen*) for the 1931 Amsterdam exhibition on Frank Lloyd Wright is pure de Stijl—intellectual, severe, emotionless.

Abstraction helped posterists develop the use of symbols. This was important because a poster had to reach the viewer's subconscious quickly in the busy twentieth-century cityscape. Symbols conveyed messages fast, and abstraction freed artists and businessmen alike from having to fill the poster with words and images. Saying more with less became the objèct. J. S. Anderson's
88 "You Can Be Sure of Shell"* (1935) juxtaposes car wheels with a group of pistons. It is a good design, but Cassandre's single symbol, the train wheels, is more effective than Anderson's two.

C. O. MÜLLER, *"Phoebus Palast,"* poster, 1929, Germany (Pat Kery Fine Arts, New York)

Symbols of material progress abound in Art Deco posters. Pyramids, stairs, and triangles stood for engineering feats already accomplished as well as those yet to be achieved. Binder's 1939 poster for the New York World's
113 Fair,* with its effective use of searchlights, airplanes, and stars, along with the famous trylon and perisphere, aptly symbolized the fair's motto, "The World of Tomorrow."

The development of commercial graphics

In the Art Deco era, commercial art became a recognized profession, and the graphic designer was born. The design philosophy developed at that time encouraged innovation, but the new design principles, in order to prevail, had to penetrate—or bypass—many established professional and social attitudes as well as personal and national traditions. They succeeded to a large extent, but far from entirely.

In the 1890s, little pressure was exerted on poster artists to go beyond producing a pleasing, attention-getting illustration. By the 1920s, advertisers demanded dynamic compositions to manipulate the public's attention and sell products, and artists responded with sophisticated new uses of page layout, typefaces, and color. One device that came to dominate poster art was the dramatic perspective, such as the aerial view, the ground-to-sky angle, and the sweeping diagonal. It created the unexpected—startling, even shocking the passerby—a must in the message-laden environment.

94 "Pianos Daudé"* (1926) effectively brings together the new graphic devices: the aerial view onto a bald-headed man playing the piano combines with the sweeping diagonal and a dynamic use of color. Interestingly, it was designed not by a professional graphic artist but by the president of the Daudé Piano Company.

Poster artists moving toward clean lines and geometric stylization found the existing typography inadequate to support the prevailing mood. Several, including Bernhard and Cassandre, designed typefaces for their posters. Most adopted the functional-looking sans-serif faces that reflected the
77 abstract style of the new art. Cassandre's "Nord Express"* exemplifies his mastery of the modern use of type. Typography makes up the border of the poster; a different typeface lists seven cities of destination, which seem to float on the tracks; and a color change at the corners of the title brings the eye up from the vanishing perspective to remind the viewer of the *Nord Express* train itself.

German innovations uniting aesthetics with industry began at the beginning of the twentieth century. In 1923, when László Moholy-Nagy arrived at the Bauhaus from Hungary to oversee the printing workshops, he noted, "We began to realize that the form, the size, the color, and the arrangement of the typographic material had a strong visual impact."[5] At the Bauhaus, Tschichold, Josef Albers, Herbert Bayer, Van Doesburg, and Schwitters experimented with typography. The Bauhaus principle "form follows function" meant that the artist's allegiance must be to the purpose of the design. What today seems simple and logical was then revolutionary. Cassandre, the most advanced of the poster designers in comprehending and using these ideas, described a poster artist's function as that of a catalyst delivering a telegraph message from point A to point B.

GILLES DE BAS, *"Renault," poster, 1925, France (Pat Kery/Jacques Mallet Fine Arts, New York)*

France and the Art Deco poster

The French stood above all others as exponents of Art Deco posters; France was the center of the modern stylistic developments, and posters were a French tradition. Four artists, dubbed "the Musketeers," led poster and advertising design in Paris during the Art Deco era: Cassandre, Loupot, Jean Carlu, and Paul Colin. Cassandre and Carlu had the more intellectual approach, using the new art principles extensively in their work. Colin and Loupot expressed the sensibilities of the French, and the Art Deco spirit, with a softer, more emotional approach.

Cassandre was the ultimate professional communicator and a pioneer in using the new visual tools of the graphic artist. Daring to defy convention, he created complex designs that to the viewer seemed visually simple, and he can be credited with transforming poster design. Born in the Ukraine, Cassandre was schooled in France, where he was strongly influenced by the avant-garde painters. His work shows elements of Cubism, Purism, Futurism, and Surrealism, as well as Constructivism. Abstraction was central to all his posters. In 1936 the Museum of Modern Art in New York held an exhibition of his posters—quite an achievement for a "secondary art." In the 1930s he moved to the United States, where he worked on a variety of graphic design projects, including advertisements, packages, and logos, as well as some outstanding covers for *Harper's Bazaar*.* During this time he was also involved in stage and costume design and easel painting.

125, 147, 300

For sheer inventiveness and originality, however, his posters were his best creations. Beginning with "Au Bûcheron" (1923), which won first prize at the 1925 Paris Exposition, when he was only twenty-two, Cassandre created one landmark poster after another. Nine classics produced in a decade were "L'Intrans"* (1925), "Nord Express"* (1927), "Étoile du Nord" (1927), "L.M.S. Bestway"* (1928), "Dr. Charpy" (1930), "Triplex"* (1930), "Dubo . . . Dubon . . . Dubonnet"* (1932), "Wagon-Bar" (1932), and "Normandie" (1935). None rests on a formula. Cassandre seemed to challenge himself, propelling himself into uncharted territory with each poster in an unceasing surge of innovation. His effective integration of typography has already been noted. In "Étoile du Nord" he mastered the vanishing perspective; in "Wagon-Bar," montage; and in "Normandie," dynamic scale changes. "Normandie" spawned hundreds of less successful imitations; his monumental ocean liner looming above eye level epitomizes this type of travel poster and captures the Art Deco spirit of grandness and power.

93/77
80/204
220

Perhaps Cassandre's most successful poster is "L'Intrans" (for the Parisian newspaper *L'Intransigeant*), which reveals his ingenuity and his power to dominate the senses. He shows a semiabstract "Marianne," symbol of the voice of France, receiving messages through telegraph wires and delivering them through her mouth. The idea is intellectual, but the effect is overpowering. To speed comprehension, Cassandre shortened both the name of the newspaper and its motto—*Le Plus Fort* was originally *Les plus fort tirages des journaux de soir* ("The evening paper with the widest circulation"). Shortening it both reminds readers of the idiom for "widest circulation" and presents the literal meaning, "the strongest." Whichever way it is read, the simplified motto is far more effective.

Cassandre took his own life in 1968, at the age of sixty-seven. A letter of rejection for a proposed new typeface lay on his desk. He died just before the poster revival of the early seventies, which hailed him as a genius.

With Maurice Moyrand, Cassandre founded an advertising agency, Alliance Graphique, in 1926, the year after his success with "L'Intrans." Loupot joined them in 1930 but was totally different in style and work habits. In contrast to Cassandre's geometric hard edge were Loupot's gentle, painterly qualities. Although subtle in his technique, Loupot was more direct than Cassandre in presenting ideas. He depicted real objects and people, as opposed to Cassandre's allusive floating windshields, telegraph wires, and railroad tracks. Nevertheless, Loupot produced a few Cubist-inspired posters, such as those for Van Heusen* in 1928 and Mira in 1929, and he did move toward a more abstract, hard-edged style during the thirty years he designed posters, packaging, and logos for St. Raphaël.*

305
2,168

The agency was disbanded in 1935, a year after Moyrand died in an automobile accident. Cassandre had moved away from posters, but Loupot contin-

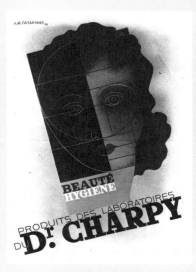

A. M. CASSANDRE, *"Dr. Charpy,"* poster, 1930, France (Posters Please, New York)

A. M. CASSANDRE, *"Étoile du Nord,"* poster, 1927, France (Posters Please, New York)

CHARLES LOUPOT, *"St. Raphaël Quinquina,"* poster on blimp, c. 1935, France (Musée de l'Affiche, Paris)

JEAN CARLU, *"Pépa Bonafé," poster, 1928, France (Musée de l'Affiche, Paris)*

96 ued to produce fine examples, such as "Twining's Tea" and "Austin Tractors." His most admired poster, however, is one of his earliest* (1920). Designed to sell automobiles, it shows a stylish red-haired woman driving a speeding car. Here was a simple concept beautifully executed, and it launched Loupot's career.

A third "Musketeer," Carlu, was as inventive as Cassandre but not as adept at delivering a message with immediate impact. He showed greater diversity in his style, however. "Désarmement" is an emotional statement against war; 112/104 "Fêtes de Paris"* presents a stylish couple at the races; "Théâtre Pigalle"* is totally abstract; "Aquarium" shows a fish reminiscent of a soft Loupot figure; and "Havana Larrañaga" (1929) depicts a cubistic man with a cigar.

145 Carlu's "Grandes Fêtes" shows a stylized, sophisticated couple who earlier had been immortalized in neon on a *Vanity Fair* * magazine cover. Many artists have tried, but with less success, to achieve the interplay and sophistication of Carlu's man and woman. In this poster, Carlu drew quick, light lines in a manner suggestive of Dufy.

Carlu adopted a variety of avant-garde techniques: symbolism, abstraction, montage, photomontage. In speeches and articles the often-quoted Carlu gave insights into his primary inspiration. He was partial to the Cubists 60 Gleizes and Juan Gris. Of his well-known poster "Pépa Bonafé"* (1928), he said in a 1980 interview: "The protector of the comédienne Pépa Bonafé asked me to create a poster but I was not, like Loupot, a posterist of women; I did not feel comfortable. However, by stylizing her profile, I immediately caught the resemblance. Pépa Bonafé did not look her best, but she understood that this poster on the walls would be excellent publicity. Again, here I have used the principles dear to Juan Gris in the colors as well as the lines. I combined curves and straight lines so that I could associate the mask of joy with the mask of sadness."[6]

"Théâtre Pigalle" (1929) is reminiscent of many Dada and Constructivist pieces, in particular Francis Picabia's abstract drawings of machines. Like the painters Léger, Picabia, Lissitzky, and Duchamp, Carlu exalted the precision and beauty of machines. Created for the theater's opening night, "Théâtre Pigalle" is an intellectual, abstract conceptualization of the theater's new lighting and machinery, reputedly the most advanced of the time. The Théâtre Pigalle was an engineering marvel, with nearly two hundred projectors to light the back curtain, three levels of movable stage, and electrically operated trapdoors. And Carlu's design was as modern as the theater.

Carlu is most remembered in France for his "Air France" and "Mon Savon" posters, which were before the public for years when he was art director of both companies. Some of his strongest posters were about politics or war, such as "Pour le Désarmement des Nations" (1932), which depicts an anguished mother with her child as the target of a bomb. Carlu himself knew the horrors of dismemberment, as his right arm had been amputated after an accident at the age of eighteen. This handicap did not seem to slow him down or prevent his working with materials, such as aluminum, copper, and neon tubing, that required cutting and shaping.

The last "Musketeer," Colin, is most remembered for his entertainment posters, although many of his nearly fifteen hundred designs were for trans-

portation, politics, and various products. He first attained fame, along
101   with his subject, with his celebrated 1925 poster "Revue Nègre,"* which
announced Josephine Baker's Paris premiere. His many posters, paintings,
and book illustrations of Baker and her musicians were classics, beautifully
capturing an important era in French music hall history. Another of Colin's
most memorable posters, "Lisa Duncan," was also designed in 1925. Colin
continued to produce posters for the music hall, theater, ballet, and opera,
and created hundreds of stage sets and costumes. In 1926 he began his École
Paul Colin, a school for graphic artists, where he taught for nearly forty
years. It is said that at the end of the school year he often treated his students
101   to an evening at the Tabarin, the subject of one of his best-known posters,*
which shows a triple image of a woman dancing the Charleston.

Compared with other categories of posters, the Art Deco entertainment
poster was influenced not so much by the avant-garde as by the style and
mood of Paris, the pleasure capital of the world. "Bal de la Couture" (1925),
created by Georges Lepape for the famous fashion ball at the Théâtre des
Champs-Élysées, sums up much of the French high style. It was produced in
1925, the year of the Paris Exposition. In it, the couple's elegance, aloofness,
and pride at being among the fashionable set are beautifully rendered.

Germany and the Art Deco poster

Fine posters were produced in Germany during the Art Deco era, although
many do not reflect the style. The Germans and the French approached
graphic art in a different manner, according to national tendencies. The
French put more emphasis on the senses and the intellect, while the Germans
admired power and emotion. German Expressionism, that country's most
important avant-garde movement, was too intense, too engrossing, to be
brought easily into the French decorative style. When a German poster
showed a couple stepping out for the evening, the mood was often one of
decadence. Performance posters tended to be wild and highly charged, with a
provocative mood or agitated position of elements to stir emotion. The
Bauhaus was a major influence in both countries, but it did not unify their
styles. Indeed, the Bauhaus was not invited to participate in the 1925 Paris
Exposition, part of the continuing reaction to World War I.

Walter Schnackenberg, Julius Engelhard, Josef Fennecker, and Ludwig
Hohlwein were some of the German artists who developed an international
style that did reflect the spirit of Art Deco. Julius Klinger, Julius Gipkins,
and Bernhard generally retained their commercial advertising style, and
some of their posters are fine examples of Art Deco. Hans Rudi Erdt might
have set the style in Germany had he not been killed in the war. His
"Problem Cigarettes" poster of 1912 is an early Art Deco work.

Fennecker produced many superb posters for the theater and cinema. They
were often dramatic and highly emotional, such as "Das Ballett der Winter-
100   saison"* (1919). Fennecker ranks with Léon Bakst as a master at depicting
movement. Engelhard had the lightest touch of the German posterists and
102   was very active in fashion illustration. His "Mode Ball"* of 1928 epitomized
the Art Deco woman—trim, chic, bold, and dressed in a daring costume
surrounded by jewels and furs. Ernst Ludwig Kirchner and Käthe Kollwitz
produced posters (like those of the Austrians Oskar Kokoschka and Egon
Schiele) with a dramatic intensity rooted in Expressionism.

PAUL COLIN, "Lisa Duncan," poster, 1925, France (Posters Please, New York)

GEORGES LEPAPE, "Bal de la Couture," poster, 1925, France (Pat Kery/Jacques Mallet Fine Arts, New York)

H. R. ERDT, "Problem Cigarettes," poster, 1912, Germany (Reinhold/Brown Gallery, New York)

The Germans at first tended to shy away from Cubist geometry, although some fine examples of geometric designs exist. *Rettet euch in den Reichsluft-schutzbund* (c. 1943) uses searchlights in the sky to form a pattern on the airplanes above. German designers, however, eventually moved toward the Bauhaus emphasis on the use of white space in design, as well as toward the abstraction of objects, as in de Stijl and Constructivism.

The poster magazine *Das Plakat* devoted an issue to each of two German posterists—Hohlwein and Schnackenberg. Hohlwein was recognized in 1913, when his career was just beginning, Schnackenberg in 1921, at the height of his powers. Stylistically, they were miles apart: Schnackenberg was decadent and risqué, Hohlwein stylish and descriptive. Hohlwein was the most popular posterist of the time, the best-known internationally, and the most prolific; Schnackenberg's art had sophistication and flair. The cover of his *Das*
150   *Plakat** issue is an excellent example: a beautiful red-haired woman, nude but for long formal yellow gloves, perches over a city at night, blowing little pieces of paper from her hand. Schnackenberg's most famous poster is
290   "Odeon Casino"* (1920), one of several he produced for that fashionable restaurant-nightclub in Berlin.

Hohlwein, too, had a unique style, aligned with neither the fashion nor the avant-garde movements. He mastered the important elements of great posters: unity, dramatic presentation, and the effective use of white space. What set him apart most, though, was his use of color. His technique involved letting colors dry to various stages before overprinting. As a result, Hohlwein's lithographs possess a wonderful transparency and look almost like watercolors, with marvelous effects of shading that no one else had achieved. He used unlikely colors; for instance, to create a mood of mystery and sophistication, one person might be colored a striking pink and another purple or green. As Alan Fern noted in his Museum of Modern Art catalogue, *Word and Image* (1968), "Hohlwein added a new dimension to
89   poster art with his mastery of brilliant colors." In "Herkules/Bier"* (c. 1925) Hohlwein was in full control of his powers. Using only brown, beige, and pink, he created an awesome, muscular man with dramatic shadows that hide his menacing face and accentuate his bulging muscles.

82   "Die Grathnohl-Zigarette"* (1921) creates another effect with a completely different type of male, the elegant top-hatted gentleman. The figure, in total shadow, is given life only by the red glow of a cigarette. It is a superbly subtle design. Hohlwein was probably the best illustrator of men in the period. (His
117   only peer was J. C. Leyendecker,* the German-born American illustrator of the Deco era.) He depicted the servant, muscleman, sportsman, gentleman, businessman, gourmand, or soldier with equal ease. In the mid-1930s, Hohlwein spent much of his time rendering mighty warriors as propaganda for Nazi war posters. His style had many emulators, as can be seen in
105   Wurbel's 1936 Olympic poster,* one of the few that equal Hohlwein's work.

Italy and the Art Deco poster

The Italians, like the Germans, fell outside the Art Deco mainstream. Their
76   best poster designer, Cappiello, moved to Paris, leaving Marcello Dudovich,* who was already in his forties when the Deco style took hold, as Italy's premier posterist. One of the major commissioners of posters in Italy was Ricordi, the publishers and printers. They commissioned Dudovich as early as 1895, and many other fine artists into the next era, including Aleardo

63

ANONYMOUS, *"Rettet euch in den Reichsluftschutzbund,"* poster, c. 1943, Germany (Jacques Mallet Fine Arts, New York)

WALTER SCHNACKENBERG, *"Anne Ecmans,"* poster, c. 1920, Germany (Jacques Mallet Fine Arts, New York)

LUDWIG HOHLWEIN, *"Kaffee Hag,"* poster, 1913, Germany (Jacques Mallet Fine Arts, New York)

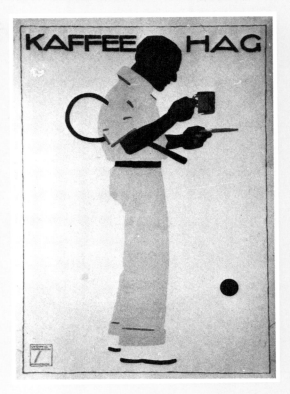

HERBERT MATTER, *"Winterferien," poster, 1934, Switzerland*
(Deborah Glusker Le Brave, Paris)

Terzi and Lucien-Achille Mauzan. The latter was a Frenchman who worked in Italy from 1909 to 1927 and then worked in South America. Mauzan's trademark was a clownlike subject with exuberant gestures, popeyes, and an elastic mouth. His style was not unlike that of Cappiello, always whimsical, in bold colors, and at times shocking in subject, like his picture of a pig looking at itself in a vanity mirror or a man with a fly on his tongue. His 81 "Sensacional Liquidacion"* for Saga ex Cooperativa in Peru is one of his best: the man with the elastic face and popping button eyes is yelling "fire sale!" as flames billow from the Saga store.

Switzerland and the Art Deco poster

No company in the world produced more high-quality posters than the Swiss clothing manufacturer PKZ. It commissioned the best Swiss posterists and many from other countries, including Hohlwein and Loupot. The PKZ logo was so well recognized that no explanation was necessary. Posters needed only to display it on a box or a coat label. Among the distinguished artists who designed PKZ posters were Otto Baumberger, Karl Bickel, Hans Falk 84 Arnhold, Alex Diggelman, Otto Morach,* Ernst Keller, and Herbert Matter. Although each had his own style, their overall tendency was toward simplicity; clean, direct, Bauhaus imagery; and no-nonsense typography.

Baumberger, signing his posters with only a *B*, was perhaps the most prolific Swiss poster artist of the period. Two of his most famous posters are the simplest, "Baumann" (1922), showing only a silk top hat, and "PKZ" (1923), with only a coat, in which he produced a dramatic impact by showing apparel larger than life. One reason for Baumberger's popularity was his incredible versatility, at various times fashionable, cubistic, humorous, or painterly.

The best of the Swiss artists was Matter, one of the few who might be considered in a class with Cassandre. He became an international force in the development of photography in the graphic arts, and his 1928 poster for PKZ* was a sign of what was to come in the technique of photomontage. It is said to have been the first montage poster, although it is illustrated without a photograph. "All Roads Lead to Switzerland"* (1935) and "Winterferien"* (1934) show the full development and force of his photomontage style. In the first poster, Matter created depth by layering the road and various mountain ranges with a tactile brick road leading to the smooth snow-covered mountains. The second example at first appears to be just a matter of laying a large face on the mountainside, with the figure looking at six skiers moving down the slopes. As in a Cassandre design, its simplicity is deceptive. Various devices—for example, the maneuvering of the skiers around the type—have been used to move the viewer's eye around the design and to the title. Matter had excellent training: he studied at the Académie Moderne in Paris under Léger in 1928 and then apprenticed with Cassandre. He also assisted Le Corbusier in architecture, exhibitions, photography, and typography. After moving to the United States in the 1930s, Matter turned to photography full time, only occasionally doing graphic design.

Great Britain and the Art Deco poster

In Great Britain, the London Underground and the British Railroad published the most important posters, with three non-British designers

OTTO BAUMBERGER, *"Marque PKZ," poster, 1923, Switzerland (Posters Please, New York)*

producing the most brilliant work: Marfurt, the Swiss artist living in Belgium; Alexander Alexeieff, the Russian living in Paris; and, most important, McKnight-Kauffer, the American who led poster design in England for decades.

79 Alexeieff's "Night Scotsman"* (1932) followed four years after Marfurt's
72 cubistic "Flying Scotsman"* (1928), which created artistic shock waves that are still felt today. Alexeieff's poster is equally good, but the airy, watercolor style does not seem to have lasting impact, although in this masterpiece he equals the exquisite color sensibility of Loupot or Hohlwein.

Born in Great Falls, Montana, far from the avant-garde, McKnight-Kauffer went to Europe at twenty-three to study art, having been inspired by the 1913 Armory Show in New York. At the outbreak of World War I he moved to London, and in 1915 he received his first commission from the London Underground, an account that kept him busy for the next quarter century, and for which he produced his most important posters. McKnight-Kauffer also created posters for the Great Western Railway, the Orient Line, and many commercial products. His "Power, Nerve Centre of London's Under-
78 ground"* (1930) demonstrated his remarkable ability. Had he maintained a more consistent level of quality, he would have achieved the stature of Cassandre. Critics today, however, generally rank him a step below.

McKnight-Kauffer was strongly affected by the avant-garde movements. He was a friend of Wyndham Lewis, and in 1920 helped try to revive interest in Lewis's Vorticist ideas. The poster that best reveals his avant-garde tendencies is "Daily Herald," first produced in 1919 as a Vorticist woodcut abstrac-
91 tion entitled "Flight of Birds."* McKnight-Kauffer returned to the United States in 1939 and died in 1951.

The success of British poster art in the Art Deco era was due in large part to Frank Pick, who, for three decades after becoming director of London Underground advertising in 1908, commissioned some of the world's most exciting graphic work. His artists included Jean Dupas, Paul Nash, Moholy-Nagy, Man Ray, André Marty, Frank Brangwyn, Joseph Pennell, and Austin Cooper. Outstanding among Pick's commissions was one in which Edward Johnston was asked to produce a new, clean-looking sans-serif alphabet for London Underground posters. Johnston's 1916 creation, called Railway, formed the basis for some of the important modern sans-serif typeface designs.

Marfurt's posters for England were rarities, as he stayed close to home in Belgium, his adopted country. He founded Les Créations Publicitaires, which for thirty years produced exceptional advertising graphics for such clients as Chrysler and Remington. Of the twenty-two Belgian posters shown at the Munich international poster exhibition in 1928, fourteen were designed by Marfurt. "Flying Scotsman" is considered his best, a powerful cubistic abstraction that creates a colorful design using the people in the crowd.

Some other European artists who produced posters with Art Deco stylization
78 were José Morell* from Spain; Binder, an Austrian who worked in America; and Magritte from Belgium. Before Magritte gained distinction as a Surreal-
176, 219, 227 ist painter, he was a magazine and advertising illustrator.* In his fashionable
294 women, as seen in his 1926 poster "Primevère,"* it is difficult to foresee his eventual unique style.

ALEXANDER ALEXEIEFF, "Dine on the L.N.E.R.," poster, 1928, Great Britain (coll. Tony Scanlon, London)

66

LEO MARFURT, "Minerva," poster, c. 1930, Belgium (Pat Kery Fine Arts, New York)

Russia, the influence of film, and the Art Deco poster

The Russian film industry in the late 1920s inspired some of the most avant-garde posters of the period. Their daring and creative ingenuity have hardly been surpassed. Sadly, this was a short-lived phenomenon, as political developments eventually discouraged experimentation.

The Stenberg brothers, Vladimir and Georgii, were the most important of these Russian posterists. They had complete control of their craft and used innovative ways of expression. "Man with a Movie Camera" (1929) is a fine example of their work. Its ground-swell view is ingeniously contrasted with a photograph of a dancer arched backward, with small circles of type that swirl into a spiral, giving the design three sets of tension. Daring in their use of photography and typography, the Stenberg brothers stood as much in the forefront as any painter of the period.

Alexander Rodchenko, one of the leaders of Russian Constructivism, abandoned painting in 1921 in favor of graphic communication. Fascinated by photography, in his designs he used unusual camera angles, photomontage, repetition, close-ups, and split images, devices derived from cinema.

Other poster artists used ideas from the budding film industry. Cassandre, again in the forefront, employed a cinematic technique in "Dubo . . . Dubon . . . Dubonnet" in 1932. (A version of the poster was produced on a fan.*) His three-part progressive film-clip type of image was used in a variety of ways for more than two decades. In this design, Cassandre produces a brilliant combination of graphics and verbal puns. A figure sits in front of his glass of Dubonnet and considers its qualities. The first part, "Dubo," brings to mind *du beau*, "beautiful." The second part, "Dubon," brings to mind *du bon*, "good." "Dubonnet," is, of course, the name of the apéritif.

The United States, Hollywood, and the Art Deco period

Considering the use of elaborate Art Deco sets and the enormous amounts of money spent on Hollywood extravaganzas and their promotion, one would expect posters for these films to be outstanding and strong in Deco style. This was far from the case, however; the exceptionally designed American film poster is a rarity. (Perhaps this was because the Hollywood studios felt that their films were better sold to a mass audience by posters realistically depicting their famous stars than by the more sophisticated designs of the European posterists.) The 1936 movie *Crack-Up* did inspire an excellent montage design. Although it shows none of the ingenuity of the Russian cinema posters, it is powerful and memorable.

America was never a center of high-quality poster design, even though many major artists moved there from Europe in the 1930s. One reason is that posters are not the most effective communication medium in a country of such size. Industry found newspapers a better advertising tool. In addition, this period saw the rise of radio, and then television, which demanded much more of the viewer's attention; not even the strongest poster could compete. Thus, the legacy of the European posters created in the Art Deco period becomes even more significant. Not only were these posters vital in linking the avant-garde and public acceptance of modernism, and important in developing modern advertising principles, but they left the world an enormously creative body of graphic work that will be difficult to surpass.

220

STENBERG BROTHERS, *"Man with a Movie Camera," poster, 1929, Russia (priv. coll.)*

ANONYMOUS, *"Crack-Up," poster, 1936, U.S.A. (Jacques Mallet Fine Arts, New York)*

TRAVEL

The Deco era's preoccupation with luxury found its fullest expression in travel—and technology responded with magnificent ocean liners and trains that both enticed and pampered the traveler. Accordingly, European posters promoting travel by train and transatlantic liner were among the most handsome, inventive, and effective of all the graphics of the period. Poster commissions by railway and steamship companies went to the best artists of the time, and they were inspired to do some of their best work. At the same time, all the elements of the Art Deco style came together in the subject—and the designers used them to the fullest.

Cassandre was supreme in this field. His finest railway posters—"Étoile du Nord,"* "L.M.S. Bestway,"* and "Nord Express"*—combine elements of Cubism, Futurism, and modern typography with his own innovations in color and dramatic perspective.

Some travel posters made good use of aerial perspective. "L.N.E.R. Harwich,"* designed by Léo Marfurt, combines this dynamic new approach with Constructivism. Two of the most impressive posters of the period are Marfurt's "Flying Scotsman"* and McKnight-Kauffer's "Underground,"* both done for the London Transport system. Marfurt created here one of the more cubistic poster designs of the period. McKnight-Kauffer captured the essence of modern dynamism and power.

59/80/77

69

72/78

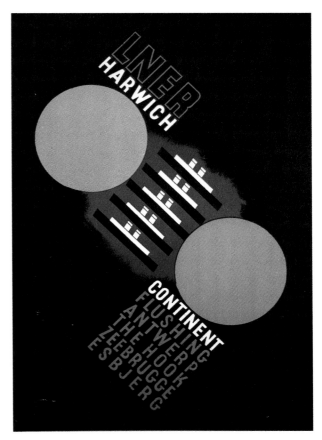

LÉO MARFURT, *"L.N.E.R. Harwich," poster, c. 1930, Belgium (Jacques Mallet Fine Arts, New York)*

WALTER HERDEG, *"St. Moritz," poster, c. 1936, Switzerland (coll. Galerie Documents, Paris)*

HERBERT MATTER, *"All Roads Lead to Switzerland," poster, 1935, Switzerland (Museum-Library, Musashino Art University, Tokyo)*

RENITAL, *"Bridlington," poster, c. 1925, Great Britain (coll. Aiden Donovan)*

LÉO MARFURT, *"Flying Scotsman," poster, 1928, Great Britain (Jacques Mallet Fine Arts, New York)*

W. F. TEN BROEK, *"Holland-Amerikalijn," poster, 1937, The Netherlands (Gilles Didier, Paris)*

KEES VAN DER LAAN, "Londen," poster, c. 1930, The Netherlands (Gilles Didier, Paris)

ALEXEY BRODOVITCH ATELIER, *"Cunard Line,"* poster, c. 1928, France (coll. Roger Coisman)

MARCELLO DUDOVICH, *"Croisières Italia,"* poster, c. 1930, Italy (coll. Brigitte Homburg)

A. M. CASSANDRE, *"Nord Express," poster, 1927, France (Nicholas Bailly, New York)*

HISUI SUGIURA, *"Only One Subway in Asia,"* poster, 1927, Japan (Museum and Archives, National Institute of Technology, Kyoto)

E. MC KNIGHT-KAUFFER, *"Power / Nerve Center of London's Underground,"* poster, 1930, Great Britain (priv. coll.)

J.-G. DOMERGUE, *"L'Été à Monté Carlo,"* poster, 1937, France (Posters Please, New York)

JOSÉ MORELL, *"Banys de Salou,"* poster, c. 1933, Spain (Nicholas Bailly, New York)

ALEXANDER ALEXEIEFF, *"The Night Scotsman," poster, 1932, Great Britain (Pat Kery/Jacques Mallet Fine Arts, New York)*

POLEFF, *"International Exhibition of Road Transportation," poster, 1934, Belgium (coll. Roger Coisman)*

A. M. CASSANDRE, *"L.M.S. Bestway," poster, 1928, France (coll. Susan J. Pack)*

SALES & PROMOTION

As early as 1903, with his first Priester matches poster, Lucien Bernhard pioneered the idea of posters that presented products and brand names simply and directly, without the profusion of messages that cluttered most designs. As seen in his "Bosch Licht"* poster, Bernhard was still using the technique in 1920.

Other artists wanted to use Bernhard's approach, but, especially in the early Deco period, they could seldom persuade advertisers, who usually felt that posters had to barrage the viewer with messages to be effective. PKZ, a men and boys' clothing store in Switzerland, was one exception, hiring excellent artists to design posters and encouraging them to use simplicity. They often used only the initials "PKZ" and a picture of clothing.* PKZ posters are some of the best, and most effective, of the period.

L.-A. MAUZAN, "Sensacional Liquidacion," poster, c. 1930, Peru (coll. Susan J. Pack)

LUDWIG HOHLWEIN, *"Die Grathnohl-Zigarette,"* poster, 1921,
Germany (Jacques Mallet Fine Arts, New York)

Die Grathnohl-Zigarette

A. M. CASSANDRE, *"Ova Reemtsma Cigaretten,"* poster, 1929, Austria-Germany (coll. Susan J. Pack)

OTTO MORACH, *"PKZ Vêtements," poster, 1923, Switzerland (Pat Kery Fine Arts, New York)*

HERBERT MATTER, *"PKZ," poster, 1928, Switzerland (Pat Kery/Jacques Mallet Fine Arts, New York)*

LAU (NICOLAU MIRALLES), *"Jean/Reputado el Mejor por los Fumadores," poster, c. 1932, Spain (Jacques Mallet Fine Arts, New York)*

KEES VAN DER LAAN, *"Leert Vliegen," poster, 1931, The Netherlands (Bernice Jackson, Boston)*

LEONETTO CAPPIELLO, *"Florio Cinzano," poster, 1930, France (Galerie 1900–2000, Paris)*

J. S. ANDERSON, *"You Can Be Sure of Shell," poster, 1935, Great Britain (coll. Tony Scanlon, London)*

WILLY WILLRAB, *"Problem Cigarettes," poster, 1926, Germany (priv. coll.)*

88

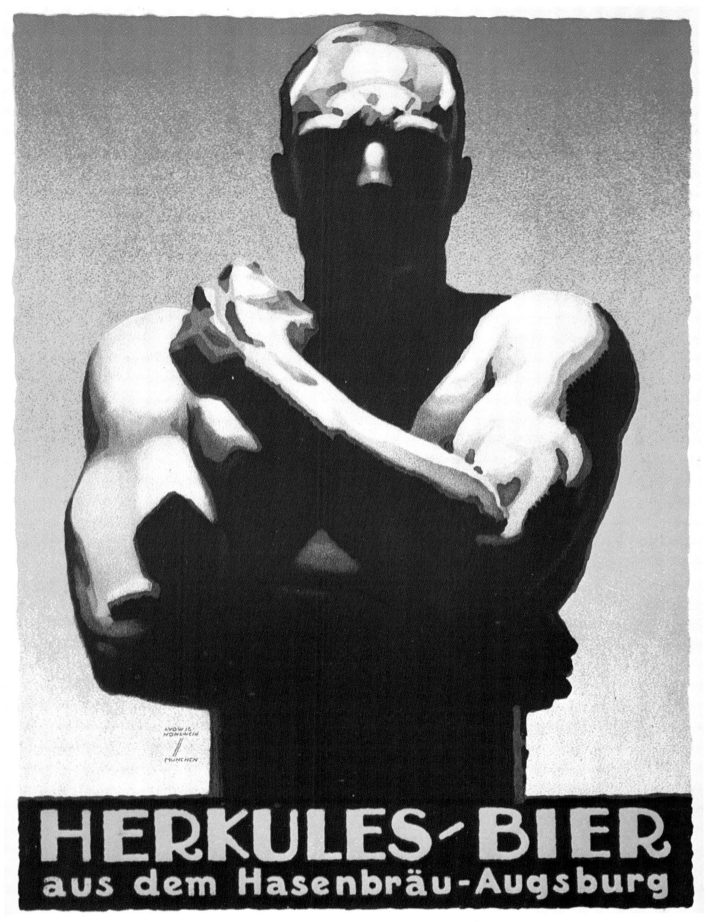

LUDWIG HOHLWEIN, *"Herkules-Bier," poster, c. 1925, Germany (Pat Kery Fine Arts, New York)*

KANEMORI SUWA, *untitled, poster, c. 1927, Japan (Shiseido Cosmetics, Tokyo)*

ERIC DE COULON, *"Grand Semaine de Tissus," poster, c. 1930, France (Reinhold/Brown Gallery, New York)*

E. MC KNIGHT-KAUFFER, *"Flight of Birds," lithograph for poster, "Daily Herald," 1919, Great Britain
(priv. coll.)*

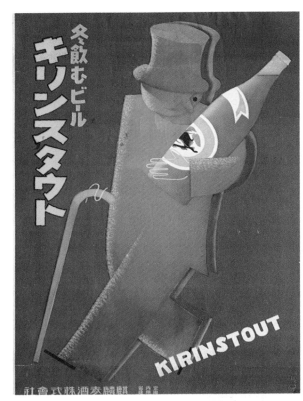

92

HOKUU TADA, *"Kirin Stout, A Winter Beer," poster, 1936, Japan (Museum-Library, Musashino Art University, Tokyo)*

REICHIRO KAWASHIMA, *untitled, poster, c. 1927, Japan (Shiseido Cosmetics, Tokyo)*

LEONETTO CAPPIELLO, *"Ca-Bloc de Remvoering," poster, 1931,*
Belgium (coll. Brigitte Homburg)

FRANÇOIS DAUDÉ, *"Pianos Daudé," poster, 1926, France (Pat Kery*
Fine Arts, New York)

FRANCIS DELAMARE, *"Union Match,"* poster, 1927, Belgium (coll. Roger Coisman)

LUCIEN BERNHARD, *"Bosch-Licht," poster, c. 1920, Germany (Jacques Mallet Fine Arts, New York)*

CHARLES LOUPOT, *"Ch. Philippossian Automobiles," poster, 1920, Switzerland (Musée de l'Affiche, Paris)*

ENTERTAINMENT

The musical revue and cabaret were at their height during the Art Deco period, and they inspired many of the great posters of the time. Some of the most magnificent were produced for Mistinguett,* who in 1926, at age fifty-seven, was still dazzling audiences at the Moulin Rouge. Part of her success was due to the people who helped create her image, like artists Erté and Zig and, more important, Charles Gesmar. Gesmar was Mistinguett's devoted and creative companion and produced many of the star's most opulent costumes, sets, and posters for about a decade, until he died in 1928.

In Germany, Walter Schnackenberg produced striking posters such as "Odeon Casino"* and "Erry & Merry."* These are among the best German works of the period. Schnackenberg's posters are highly stylized in the German manner and convey the typical mood of decadence of the time.

In a few short years during the late 1920s, Russia produced the best film posters of the era. Alexander Rodchenko was central to that flurry of activity. Like most of the avant-garde cinema posterists in Russia, Rodchenko pioneered in the use of photomontage. Some of the most imaginative cinema posters were produced by the Stenberg brothers, Vladimir and Georgii. Their posters demonstrate a mastery of Constructivism as well as photomontage. Among their best works is "Man with a Movie Camera."*

MACIEJ NOWICKI AND STANISLAWA SANDECKA, *"International Dance Competition," poster, 1933 Poland (coll. C. Zagrodzki)*

ANTHONY GIRBAL, *"Alexander Vedette Columbia,"* poster, 1937,
France (coll. Galerie Documents, Paris)

WALTER SCHNACKENBERG, *"Erry & Merry,"* poster, c. 1920, Germany
(priv. coll.)

PAUL COLIN, *"André Renaud," poster, 1929, France (Pat Kery/Jacques Mallet Fine Arts, New York)*

OTTO ARPKE, *"Reklame Ball," poster, 1928, Germany (Jacques Mallet Fine Arts, New York)*

JOSEF FENNECKER, *"Das Ballett," poster, 1919, Germany (Jacques Mallet Fine Arts, New York)*

JULIUS ENGELHARD, *"Mode Ball," poster, 1928, Germany (Posters Please, New York)*

AUGUSTE HERBIN, *"Bal de la Grande Ourse," poster, 1925, France (Posters Please, New York)*

EVENTS

Posters are especially suited to the announcement of local events such as
exhibitions, concerts, and sports. Not surprisingly, exhibitions in the arts
inspired some of the most interesting posters of the period, with many reflecting the Art Deco style. In 1929, El Lissitzky created "USSR Russische
110 Ausstellung"* for an exhibition of Russian art in Zurich. It depicts two
young people facing the future, and functions as a propaganda instrument as
well as an exhibition poster.

Outstanding posters were created also for sporting events, such as the 1936
Olympics in Germany and the Grand Prix automobile races in Switzerland.
105 Wurbel's "Olympische Spiele,"* for example, combines Constructivist
tension, cubistic collage, and a painting style reminiscent of Hohlwein.

WURBEL, *"Olympische Spiele Berlin," poster, 1936, Germany
(Musée de l'Affiche, Paris)*

TADEUSZ GRONOWSKI, *"10th Anniversary of the Polish-Soviet War,"*
poster, 1930, Poland (coll. G. Zagrodzki)

BERTHOLD LÖFFLER, *"Kunstschau Wien," poster, 1908, Austria (Pat Kery Fine Arts, New York)*

KOLOMAN MOSER, *"XIII Ausstellung," poster, 1902, Austria*
(Museum and Archives, National Institute of Technology, Kyoto)

HERMANN KEIMEL, *"Muenchner Plakat Kunst," poster, 1931, Germany (priv. coll.)*

PIERRE BELLENGER, *"Exposition d'Organisation Commerciale,"*
poster, 1929, France (coll. Pierre Bellenger)

VILMOS HUSZAR, *"Tentoonstelling,"* poster, 1929, The Netherlands
(coll. Tony Scanlon, London)

EL LISSITZKY, *"USSR Russische Ausstellung Zurich,"* poster, 1929,
Russia (priv. coll.)

MARCELLO NIZZOLI, *"XII Fiera de Milano,"* poster, 1931, Italy
(Pat Kery/Jacques Mallet Fine Arts, New York)

ANONYMOUS, *"International Exposition," poster, 1940, Japan (Museum and Archives, National Institute of Technology, Kyoto)*

JEAN CARLU, *"Grandes Fêtes de Paris," poster, 1934, France (Musée de l'Affiche, Paris)*

JEAN DUPAS, *"15ième Salon des Artistes," poster, 1927, France (Pat Kery Fine Arts, New York)*

JOSEPH BINDER, *"New York World's Fair/The World of Tomorrow," poster, 1939, U.S.A. (Hochschule für Angewandte Kunst, Vienna)*

RUPRECHT, *"Grand Prix d'Europe Autos,"* poster, 1948, Switzerland (Pat Kery/Jacques Mallet Fine
Arts, New York)

DJO BOURGEOIS, *"L'Inhumaine," poster, 1925, France (Reinhold/
Brown Gallery, New York)*

116

LUCIEN BERNHARD (BERNHARD/ROSEN ATELIER), *"Reklame Schau,"* poster, 1929, Germany (Pat Kery Fine
Arts, New York)

Magazines

In the final decade of the nineteenth century, the Western world experienced an enormous surge in magazine publication, a development that paralleled the rise in the production of posters. Magazines became the main source of popular entertainment, with as yet no competition from radio, cinema, or television. Often referred to as "little posters," magazine covers carried many of the most exciting illustrations produced.

By the turn of the century, however, the passion for these publications had already begun to wane in Europe. Most of the magazines were attached to the Art Nouveau style, in which interest was fading. Many of the best publications, such as France's *L'Estampe Originale*, *La Revue Blanche*, and *L'Assiette au Beurre*, Germany's *Jugend, Pan,* and *Simplicissimus*, Austria's *Ver Sacrum*, and Spain's *Blanco y Negro*, closed down or were much diminished in the first few decades of the new century.

In the United States a different situation unfolded. There, the magazine industry kept growing steadily. This growth was due in large part to the vast size of the country. Sent by mail to the smaller cities and rural areas outside the major publishing centers, magazines became the best way to reach a national audience.

U.S. publishers approached the founding of new journals with zest. With a spirit reminiscent of the pioneers, full of experimentation and a desire to break new ground, they built vast empires. They realized that great profits could be theirs through reaching vast numbers of people and expanding their advertising. They understood that illustration was the path to large circulation, and were fully committed to it. Illustrators became stars: Charles Dana Gibson, J. C. Leyendecker, James Montgomery Flagg, Howard Chandler Christy, and Maxfield Parrish achieved unprecedented celebrity. The sums paid for their work were enormous amounts of money for the time: in 1903 Gibson received $1,000—the equivalent of about $11,000 today—for one drawing.

In spite of this enormous success for the U.S. magazine industry as a whole, mass-audience acceptance of the Art Deco style followed relatively slowly in all publications except a few fashion magazines. Most of the illustrators retained a traditional style, with only a few, like Flagg and Leyendecker, moving into the style of the new age. (Leyendecker is perhaps best known as the illustrator of the Arrow collar ads, in which he created the character that epitomized the American Art Deco man. Leyendecker's male figures were not as sophisticated as the French men or as decadent as the Germans, but rather like handsome shiny-cheeked mannequins.)

J. C. LEYENDECKER, *untitled magazine illustration, c. 1928, U.S.A.* (priv. coll.)

Fashion magazines

The development of modernist graphic style in magazines in France and the United States was an entirely different matter when it came to fashion publications. These were in the forefront, bringing modernist ideas to the public as early as 1912, a decade before posters were to do the same.

Women's role in society was undergoing radical change, perhaps more rapidly than at any other time in history. Magazine publishers moved quickly to acknowledge the growing independence of women and to further inspire and educate them. However, even limited liberation did not come about immediately for the majority of women, and a dichotomy developed in women's publications. New, stylish fashion magazines arose that helped women develop their intellect as well as their taste, while the traditional women's publications remained sentimental and mediocre.

At the turn of the century fashion illustration was functional, realistic, uninspired, and uninspiring. Between 1908 and 1912 Parisian couturier Paul Poiret commissioned artists to illustrate his flamboyant clothing designs using a new, elongated, simplified style, and thus led the departure from traditional modes of fashion illustration toward a modernist sensibility.

Some of these illustrations were published in small books or albums in which the pictures were reproduced by pochoir, a method providing extraordinary fidelity and brilliance (see "Books"). Although privately printed—they were intended mainly for Poiret's clients—these albums did not escape the attention of the magazine industry. The new style introduced by Poiret was soon adopted in French and American magazines alike and, somewhat slowly, in other European countries. In 1912 the French *Journal des Dames et des Modes* and *La Gazette du Bon Ton* were founded, using the same illustration style and printing method as Poiret's books. In 1913 the already existing American publications *Vogue* and *Vanity Fair* followed, having been revamped by publisher Condé Nast to feature the new illustrations. (They were not printed by pochoir, since the much larger print runs of the American publications made the use of such a handwork process impractical.) These fashion magazines and others were uniform only in their commitment to the new illustration style and to the illustrators themselves.

The artists depicting fashion in the 1910s were much in demand in France and America, and most worked for all of the leading fashion publications simultaneously. It was through fashion magazines that Art Deco was brought to America, and it was they who most strongly supported the style.

La Gazette du Bon Ton, under the leadership of publisher Lucien Vogel, was the most luxurious and beautifully illustrated of the fashion magazines in this century. Vogel searched for fresh illustrative talent and assembled an impressive group of artists, including Georges Lepape, George Barbier, Erté, Charles Martin, Robert Bonfils, Pierre Brissaud, André Marty, Étienne Drian, Marthe Romme, Umberto Brunelleschi, and Eduardo Garcia Benito. Martin's illustration for the *Gazette*, "La Femme à L'Émeraude" (c. 1915), captured the spirit of the second decade of the twentieth century. His self-assured, rather carefree woman, shown in a lush forest of fantasy, is depicted in an elongated, simplified, stylized manner, with geometricism in the shapes and positions of ferns. Of all the leading fashion illustrators, Martin was the one most influenced by Cubist geometricism. By 1925 his style was as cubistic

CHARLES MARTIN, *"La Femme à L'Émeraude,"* La Gazette du Bon Ton *magazine cover, c. 1915, France (priv. coll.)*

as that of Laboureur, the artist who perhaps best blended the avant-garde art movements and commercial graphics.

When *La Gazette du Bon Ton* closed in 1925, *Femina* succeeded it as France's most important fashion magazine and became a consistent source of exciting Art Deco covers.

Condé Nast was an impressive American publishing entrepreneur with international ambitions. In 1913 he set out to revitalize *Vogue* and *Vanity Fair*, two magazines that dated from the nineteenth century, and succeeded in placing his publications at the nexus of the flow of fashion ideas between Europe and North America. *Vanity Fair* (originally named *Dress and Vanity Fair*) was then a fashion publication, but it evolved into a general entertainment magazine by the mid-1920s. For several years the covers of *Vogue* and *Vanity Fair* seemed interchangeable, with both using the best European and American fashion illustrators.

Vogue became a favorite with Europeans, as they could see in its pages the best presentation of ideas originated by their own fashion designers. In 1916, during World War I, *Vogue* began a British edition when German submarines posed a threat to the importation of copies from America. A French edition followed in 1922, and shortly after that German and Italian editions were introduced.

A few American magazine illustrators emerged, such as George Wolf Plank, Helen Dryden, Rita Senger, and E. M. A. Steinmetz, who had talents to rival their European counterparts. Plank was the most inventive. His *Vogue* cover of April 15, 1916, is a double image. At first glance, the woman popping out of the box seems to be offering a baby chick in her palm. Upon closer inspection, however, the chick can be seen as the hair of a woman who is leaning to the left with her arms outstretched. It is interesting to note that this playful presentation appeared during World War I, and that Plank's geometric treatment of the skirt and box precedes by about five years the widespread use of geometricism in graphics.

Besides Condé Nast, Time, Inc., and Hearst Publications emerged as vast publishing empires. Hearst owned *Harper's Bazaar*[7], which became *Vogue*'s archrival. *Harper's Bazaar* signed Erté, who had been designing *Vogue* covers, to an exclusive ten-year contract in 1915 and extended it for another
127 ten. He had turned out some 240 cover designs* and a reported 2,500 illustrations for various Hearst publications by 1937, when he resigned in a dispute with *Bazaar* editor Carmel Snow.

Elsewhere in Europe, fashion magazines did not match the French and American commitment to Art Deco graphic design in the 1910s. By the mid-
126 to late 1920s, however, German fashion publications, especially *Die Dame*,* offered beautifully stylish covers in the Deco mode. Although the Scandinavian countries were generally not attuned to the Art Deco style, a 1925 cover
142 for the Danish magazine *Tik Tak** designed by Sven Brasch stands as a noteworthy exception.

Entertainment and travel magazines

Great Britain never developed its magazine industry as much as might have been expected. Much of its creative graphic energy went into book production. Popular publications such as *The Graphic*, and even *Radio Times*,

G. W. PLANK, Vogue *magazine cover, April 15, 1916, U.S.A. (priv. coll.)*

avoided modernism in illustration, although *The Sketch* had a few interesting covers. *Punch*, England's most famous and oldest publication, only comparatively recently moved to change its cover with each issue. It ran the same Punch and Judy drawing for more than a century.

French publications tended to be either large and luxurious or very small with poor-quality paper. In either case, they were generally profusely illustrated. Three outstanding examples of French art and entertainment publications from the nineteenth century that survived World War I are *La Vie Parisienne*, *Le Rire*, and *L'Illustration*. The first, dating from 1863, finally closed its doors in 1939, after several demises and rebirths, having been in the early twenties a vehicle for some of the most titillating and risqué Art Deco illustration. It featured the illustrations of Maurice Millière and Mathilde Angeline Hérouard, frequently of sensuous women in revealing costumes. The December 6, 1919, cover of *La Vie Parisienne*, by A. Vallée, produced at the height of Art Deco stylization, utilized elements that had come to characterize the style, while exhibiting a typical concentration on lightly erotic and mildly shocking subject matter. *Le Rire*, too, published much early Deco illustration.

132, 138
133Some powerful and imaginative cover graphics were produced in Italy during the Deco period, especially in magazines such as *La Revista*, *Italia*,* and *Italie Voyages*.* In a cover of about 1930 for *La Revista*, Paolo Garretto demonstrated the power of perspective. The boxer in the foreground, towering and muscular, dominates by his size. Garretto enhanced his dominance with a strategically placed triangle representing the boxing ring. The perspective creates an illusion of distance, and makes the boxer in the background seem even smaller and weaker.

In the United States, an entertainment magazine of the first order appeared at the zenith of Art Deco activity. *The New Yorker*, first published in February 1925, was a unique magazine: sophisticated, humorous, elitist, and intellectual. Its first cover, Rea Irvin's drawing of a man with a top hat and monocle, was distinctly Art Deco in style and has been repeated annually on the anniversary of the publication's founding.

Rose Silver (Lisa Rhana) was one of the *New Yorker*'s leading cover artists with a Deco style. On a 1931 cover, Silver portrayed an elegant chanteuse in the French elongated manner. During the 1930s the *New Yorker* covers moved away from Deco style toward sophisticated cartoons, but the inside pages continued to reflect a Deco look, having retained the initial typography and Irvin's original illustrations for the department headings. Protective of its traditions and committed to promoting illustration, *The New Yorker* is the only major magazine besides *Punch* that still uses cover illustrations rather than photography. In fact, it has run only one photograph on its editorial pages since it began.

In 1913 Condé Nast asked Frank Crowninshield to run *Vanity Fair*. By 1925 the magazine had changed to a general entertainment publication. Gossipy, theatrical, intellectual, playful, and, of course, fashionable, it epitomized the Art Deco spirit of the twenties and thirties. Its covers were so popular that they inspired *Vanity Fair* cover parties, to which women came dressed in cover-related costumes. At the same time, Crowninshield gave the magazine an ever-widening international scope and ever-expanding political appeal, thereby attracting male readers as well. Without doubt, the success of *Vanity*

CHARLES LABORDE, Le Rire *magazine cover, August 15, 1931, France (priv. coll.)*

A. VALLÉE, La Vie Parisienne *magazine cover, December 6, 1919, France (priv. coll.)*

PAOLO GARRETTO, La Rivista *magazine cover, c. 1930, Italy (coll. Paolo Garretto)*

ROSE SILVER, The New Yorker *magazine cover, February 24, 1931, U.S.A. (priv. coll.)*

Fair was due to the genius of Crowninshield. A noted art collector and a founder of the Museum of Modern Art, he helped disseminate the new ideas of the era by spotlighting Picasso, Braque, Pascin, Modigliani, Steichen, and other pioneers of art in the magazine.

Miguel Covarrubias and Garretto were regular contributors to *Vanity Fair* and were the most impressive of the Art Deco–style magazine illustrators in America. Covarrubias arrived in New York in 1923 from Mexico at the age of eighteen and won success immediately with his caricatures of prominent people. With a charming mischievousness that probed his subjects' character, Covarrubias's illustrations straddled entertainment and acerbity, as can be

128 seen in his famous cover portrayal of Greta Garbo.* A popular feature in *Vanity Fair* was "Impossible Interviews," imaginary meetings of such unlikely pairs as Freud and Jean Harlow or Stalin and John D. Rockefeller, which gave Covarrubias an opportunity to show his skill in caricature with
141 his geometric Deco style.*

Garretto also was a fine caricaturist. A typical example is his characterization of Gandhi, which shows the artist's cleverness, insight, and mastery of geometric stylization. Garretto portrayed Gandhi from two perspectives simultaneously. In a simplified, geometric, quite abstract drawing the Indian leader appears as a "man of the people." On one lens of Gandhi's spectacles Garretto superimposed a cartoon of Ghandhi as a statesman, dressed in top hat and tails. The impact is immediate and powerful. Garretto proved more versatile than Covarrubias and developed a broader international following, working for many Italian, French, and American publications.

An American magazine with some of the most handsome, imaginative Art Deco covers was, curiously, *Asia*, a small-circulation magazine about a part of the world where Deco had little impact. Beginning in 1924, for about a decade, *Asia* owner Willard Straight published a series of Deco covers, most by Frank McIntosh, that were among the most exciting in the world. One McIntosh cover brilliantly juxtaposes images of modernism—a sleek modern skyscraper and expensive automobile—and traditionalism—an Asian-style building and a rickshaw. In June 1932 McIntosh created another beautiful cover design with a woman's elongated fingers spanning almost the entire
137 page.* The effect is startling. Surprisingly, *Asia* did not modernize its inside page design and rarely ran an inside picture in color.

Some illustrators specialized in portraying the flapper of the 1920s, the best
134 being Fish (Anne H. Sefton) and John Held, Jr.* Held drew cartoonlike figures and accompanied his illustrations with amusing captions. Fish regularly contributed drawings in Deco style to *Vanity Fair* and other magazines. The June 1923 cover of *Vanity Fair* shows the style at its best.

Business, political, and news magazines

Henry Luce was a trendsetter in magazine publishing. In 1923 he introduced *Time*, a "news capsule," to compete with the new radio medium. In 1930 he introduced *Fortune*, the first business publication with high aesthetic standards, and in 1936 came *Life* and photojournalism.

Fortune was a sumptuous creation in its first two decades, printed on heavy paper and mailed in a presentation box. It was published at an unprecedented one dollar per copy just one month after the stock market crash in

121

PAOLO GARRETTO, Vanity Fair *magazine cover, November 1931, U.S.A. (priv. coll.)*

FRANK MCINTOSH, Asia *magazine cover, April 1932, U.S.A. (priv. coll.)*

FISH, Vanity Fair *magazine cover, June 1923, U.S.A. (priv. coll.)*

1929. Its commitment to graphic quality was one of the reasons for its survival through the world economic crisis. *Fortune* covers were some of the most beautiful and original of the Deco period, often influenced by Futurism's fascination with industry and speed. The cover artists were outstanding, and included Diego Rivera, Ben Shahn, Léger,* Garretto,* Binder,* and Anthony Petrucelli.

146/140/129

The cover of the February 1932 issue of *Fortune* was Garretto's arresting aerial view of smokestacks. It was a convincing demonstration of his understanding of the new use of perspective and other vanguard graphic design techniques of the period. The cover in January 1937—Petrucelli's large

135   Champagne glasses*—demonstrates *Fortune*'s apparent policy of allowing artists broad freedom of expression, whether or not the result related directly to business themes.

Many of the most important German publications of the Art Deco era, including the famous *Simplicissimus, Illustrierte Zeitung, Fliegende Blätter, Kladderadatsch*, and *Lustige Blätter*, had a political or satirical slant, and not much Deco stylization. Inferior-quality paper and printing were a problem for these and many other German publications during these troubled years. *Die Woche* frequently had clever two-color Deco covers in the 1930s, but by this time Deco was waning, and these are not the most impressive examples of the style. *Die Woche*'s April 1932 cover by VOH is one of its most memorable. As in many German illustrations, the geometry is in the construction—here, the car is angled across the page—rather than in the execution of figures and objects.

Spain produced some excellent graphics during the Deco era, mostly in *Blanco y Negro* magazine. This publication dated from the 1890s, when its commitment to graphics was very strong. In the 1920s, although generally

131   not as graphically interesting, it ran some striking modernist covers.* By the 1970s it had evolved into Spain's main news magazine, with little remaining graphic value except for regular reprints of old illustrations.

Art and graphics magazines

Magazine publishing in the Art Deco period involved the many publications that gave impassioned support to the emerging art movements. These magazines profoundly affected the graphics in the popular journals of the time. Artists and art directors were eager to incorporate the vanguard ideas into their work. Where the United States was predominant in fashion, general-interest, and popular magazines, the Europeans monopolized art-related publishing.

Art-movement magazines were generally issued in small quantities. Several publications were associated with Dadaism—*291, 391, 691*, and *Dadaphone*

26   —with such leading artists as Picabia* and Braque providing cover designs. In 1914 *Blast** documented Wyndham Lewis's Vorticism. A decade later

156   Lewis published a few issues of *The Enemy*,* displaying his ability to weave a fragmented array of color and words into an effective whole. Lissitzky illus-

154   trated and produced a number of avant-garde publications, including *Vesch** *Nos. 1–2*, the first pro-Soviet periodical in the West, which was published briefly in Berlin in 1922.

There were also important de Stijl and Surrealist publications, as well as

152/26   "little publications": *Transition, Broom,** and *The Little Review** (later *The*

PAOLO GARRETTO, Fortune *magazine cover, February 1932, U.S.A.* *(priv. coll.)*

VOH, Die Woche *magazine cover, April 23, 1932, Germany* *(priv. coll.)*

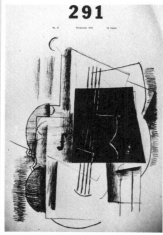

GEORGES BRAQUE, 291 *magazine cover, November 1915, U.S.A.* *(priv. coll.)*

Paris Review). Typically in a small format, these vanguard magazines ran covers by such notable artists as Kandinsky, Duchamp, Arp, Klee, Miró, Léger, and Man Ray.

150, 153, 154

151
Among publications that focused on commercial graphic art, France's *Arts et Métiers Graphiques* and *Arts Ménagers* and Germany's *Das Plakat** and *Gebrauchsgraphik** were beautifully presented. They reproduced all kinds of graphics: stamps, postcards, posters, packages, ads, wallpapers, and prints, often in facsimile.

10
One of the most handsome and consistently intriguing of this kind of publication was *Wendingen*, an architectural magazine from the Netherlands, published by H. T. Wyedveld between 1918 and 1931. *Wendingen* covers were woodcuts and lithographs, with unique modernist designs spreading across the front and back of the magazine. It used a striking square format, was printed on high-quality paper, and was finished with a Japanese book binding tied with a ribbon. Inside, every page had a gray Art Deco border. Lissitzky produced *Wendingen*'s most famous cover, for the 1921 number 11 issue.*

L'Illustration kept its importance and stylishness throughout the Art Deco period, its interior yielding some of the most exciting graphic images to be seen, many of them black-and-white ads by such designers as Cassandre, Carlu, Marty, and Lepape.

A. STAAL, Wendingen *magazine cover, XI, No. 5, 1930, The Netherlands (John Vloemans Antiquarian Books, The Hague)*

The thirties

Magazines changed radically in America in the 1930s, owing largely to the work of two Russian art directors, Mehemed Agha and Alexey Brodovitch, artists of exceptional ability and vision. In 1929 Condé Nast appointed Agha art director of *Vogue* in New York, where he introduced a radical new practice to American magazine publishing: the participation of the art director in all visual matters. Under Agha, the publication was designed as a unified whole, rather than illustrations and design being considered separately. *Vanity Fair* was transformed as well.

An imaginative photographer himself, Agha introduced many of the great modern photographers to the pages of *Vogue* and *Vanity Fair*, among them Edward Steichen, Cecil Beaton, Horst P. Horst, George Hoyningen-Huene, and Charles Sheeler. He introduced European modernist graphic style, with sans-serif typefaces and a creative use of space. His innovations changed the look of American magazines and inspired artists to adopt the new style.

76, 178, 180
Brodovitch* was one of the most gifted graphic artists of the period, on a par with Cassandre, but he submerged his own design career to teach and direct others. In Paris he designed sets for the Ballets Russes and did page designs for *Arts et Métiers Graphiques*. In 1930 he moved to the United States as guest of the Philadelphia Museum of Art, which was creating an advertising art department and museum school. In 1934 *Harper's Bazaar* editor Carmel Snow engaged Brodovitch to design her publication. Like Agha, he brought in the modernist European style and introduced important photographers and illustrators, including Richard Avedon, Irving Penn, Cartier-Bresson, Bérard, Cocteau, Cassandre, and Saul Steinberg. With Brodovitch at *Harper's Bazaar* and Agha at *Vogue*, the two greatest American fashion magazines were again on a par and at war with each other.

Both art directors brought more photography into their pages, which thereby evolved away from the Art Deco style, The early photographs retained a Deco feeling, as in Steichen's first *Vogue* cover, in 1932. The angles are in the geometric mode, there is modernist simplification, and the bathing beauty with the ball is backlit, giving her a characteristic Deco feeling of transformed reality. However, when *Life* was introduced in 1936, illustration was pronounced old-fashioned and the new realistic, photographic method of presentation took hold. A few magazine illustrators, such as George Petty and Alberto Vargas, made their careers in the late 1930s and 1940s, but their style was too realistic for Art Deco. The Deco era passed, but the innovations of the period marked the magazine industry with a sense of graphic form and vitality that remain today.

EDWARD STEICHEN, Vogue *magazine cover, July 1932, U.S.A. (priv. coll.)*

POPULAR MAGAZINES

A. M. CASSANDRE, Harper's Bazaar *magazine cover, March 1938, U.S.A. (priv. coll.)*

HOFMAN, The New Yorker *magazine cover, April 18, 1925, U.S.A.*
(priv. coll.)

ANONYMOUS, Die Woche *magazine cover, June 25, 1932, Germany*
(priv. coll.)

SYNTON G. RIMKI, Vanity Fair *magazine cover, January 1929, U.S.A.*
(priv. coll.)

LÉON BENIGNI, Die Dame *magazine cover, May 1935, Germany*
(priv. coll.)

ERTÉ, Harper's Bazaar *magazine cover, July 1934, U.S.A.*
(priv. coll.)

MIGUEL COVARRUBIAS, Vanity Fair *magazine cover, February 1932, U.S.A. (coll. Barbara Siegel and Walter Szykitka)*

JOSEPH BINDER, Fortune *magazine cover, December 1937, U.S.A. (priv. coll.)*

HELEN DRYDEN, Vogue *magazine cover, January 15, 1922, U.S.A.*
(priv. coll.)

G. W. PLANK, Vogue *magazine cover, June 15, 1917, U.S.A.*
(priv. coll.)

VALERIGH, Blanco y Negro *magazine cover, c. 1930, Spain (*Blanco y Negro, *Spain)*

ANONYMOUS, Turismo Uruguay *magazine cover, 1938, Uruguay*
(priv. coll.)

W. FELINI, Italia *magazine cover, 1938, Italy (priv. coll.)*

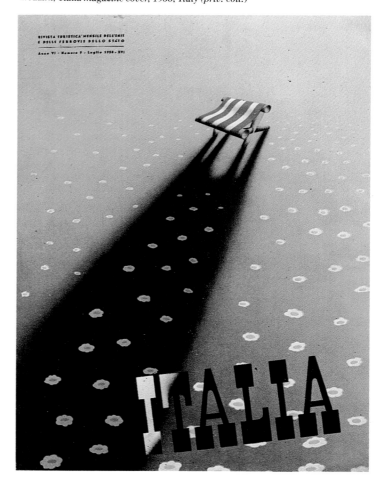

ANONYMOUS, Italie Voyages *magazine cover, July 1933, Italy (Musée des Arts Décoratifs, Paris)*

JOHN HELD, JR., *"Teaching Old Dogs New Tricks,"* Life *magazine cover, February 18, 1926, U.S.A. (priv. coll.)*

VALD'ES, *"Beau Teint Mondain,"* magazine illustration for La Vie Parisienne, *c. 1925, France (priv. coll.)*

WILLIAM WELSH, *"Summer"* Woman's Home Companion magazine cover, July 1931, U.S.A. (priv. coll.)

A. BIRNBAUM, Stage *magazine cover, October 1936, U.S.A. (priv. coll.)*

ROSE SILVER, The New Yorker *magazine cover, July 11, 1931, U.S.A.*
(priv. coll.)

ANTONIO PETRUCELLI, Fortune *magazine cover, January 1937, U.S.A.*
(priv. coll.)

MIKHAIL LARIONOV, Zhar-Ptitsa *magazine cover, 1925, no. 12.*
France-Germany (priv. coll.)

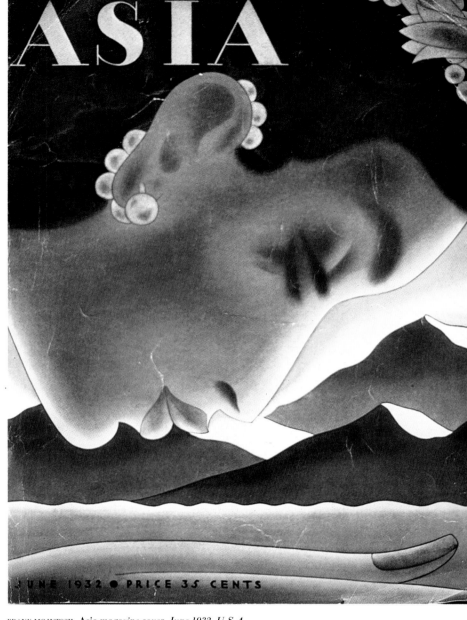

FRANK MCINTOSH, Asia *magazine cover, June 1932, U.S.A.*
(priv. coll.)

GEIS, Jugend *magazine cover, 1928, Germany (priv. coll.)*

GEORGES LEPAPE, Vogue *magazine cover, June 1, 1918, U.S.A.*
(priv. coll.)

ANONYMOUS, Italia *magazine cover, August 1936, Italy (Musée des*
Arts Décoratifs, Paris)

FRANK MCINTOSH, **Asia** *magazine cover, November 1929, U.S.A. (priv. coll.)*

PAOLO GARRETTO, **Fortune** *magazine cover, August 1932, U.S.A. (priv. coll.)*

MIGUEL COVARRUBIAS, Vanity Fair *magazine illustration ("Impossible Interview: Fritz Kreisler/Louis Armstrong"), c. 1930, U.S.A. (priv. coll.)*

GEORGE BARBIER, Femina *magazine cover, November 1922, France (priv. coll.)*

WILLIAM WELSH, *"Winter"* Woman's Home Companion *magazine cover, February 1931, U.S.A. (priv. coll.)*

SVEN BRASCH, Tik Tak *magazine cover, 1925, Denmark (The Exhumation, Princeton, New Jersey)*

E. G. BENITO, Vogue *magazine cover, 1927, U.S.A. (priv. coll.)*

GEORGES LEPAPE, Vogue *magazine cover, March 15, 1927, U.S.A. (priv. coll.)*

FRANK MC INTOSH, Asia *magazine cover, October 1930, U.S.A. (priv. coll.)*

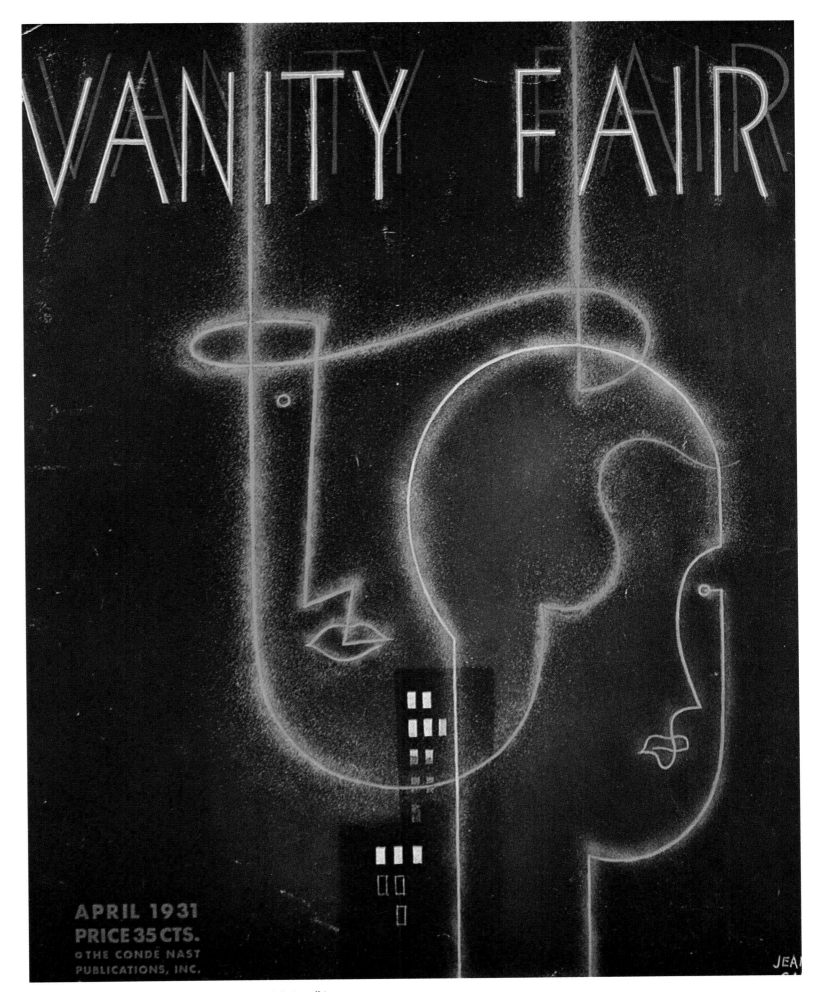

JEAN CARLU, **Vanity Fair** *magazine cover, April 1931, U.S.A. (priv. coll.)*

FERNAND LÉGER, Fortune *magazine cover, December 1941, U.S.A.*
(priv. coll.)

FRANK MC INTOSH, Asia *magazine cover, December 1931, U.S.A.*
(priv. coll.)

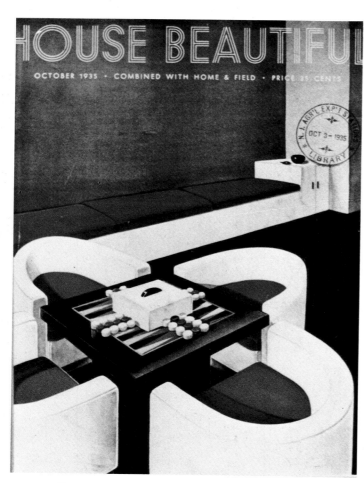

ANONYMOUS, House Beautiful *magazine cover, October 1935, U.S.A.*
(priv. coll.)

KEN, Shukan Asahi *magazine cover, August 1937, Japan (Library of
Congress, Washington)*

A. M. CASSANDRE, Harper's Bazaar *magazine cover, October 1938, U.S.A. (priv. coll.)*

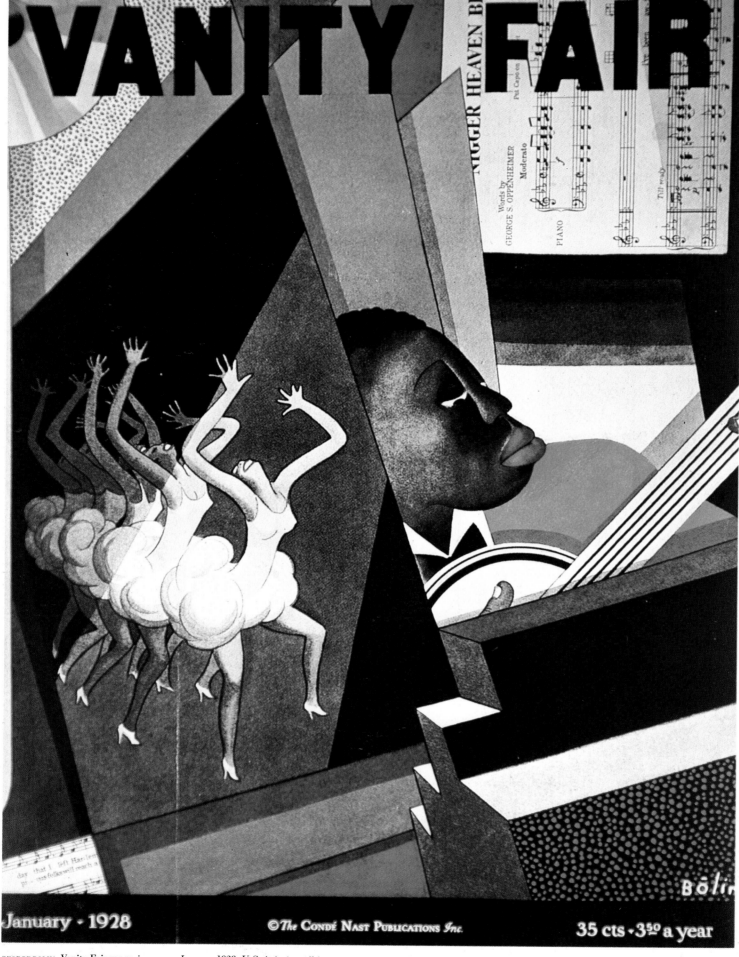

GEORGE BOLIN, Vanity Fair *magazine cover, January 1928, U.S.A. (priv. coll.)*

ANONYMOUS, *Amerikaansche Filmkunst* magazine cover, no. 7, The
Netherlands (coll. Jacques Mallet)

WALTER SCHNACKENBERG, Das Plakat *magazine cover, January 1921,*
Germany (priv. coll.)

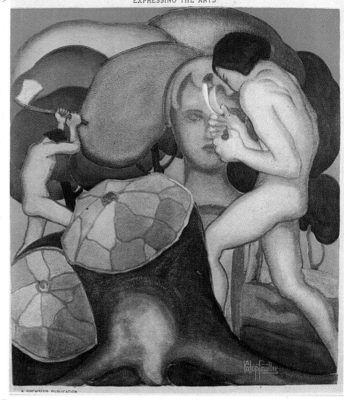

A. M. HOPFMÜLLER, Shadowland *magazine cover, c. 1932, U.S.A.*
(coll. Barbara Siegel and Walter Szykitka)

150

JOSEPH BINDER, Gebrauchsgraphik *magazine cover, May 1935, Germany (priv. coll.)*

VILMOS HUSZAR, Wendingen *(Diego Rivera issue), magazine cover, 1929, The Netherlands (John Vloemans Antiquarian Books, The Hague)*

EL LISSITZKY, Broom *magazine cover, vol. 4, c. 1923 (priv. coll.)*

WALTER KAMPMANN, Das Plakat *magazine cover, June 1921, Germany (coll. Jacques Mallet)*

EL LISSITZKY, Vesch *magazine cover, March–April 1922, Germany (priv. coll.)*

WALTER KAMPMANN, Das Plakat *magazine illustration, June 1921, Germany (coll. Jacques Mallet)*

JOSEPH BINDER, Graphis *magazine cover, 1948, issue no. 23, Switzerland (priv. coll.)*

CARL S. JUNGE, Inland Printer *magazine cover, February 1917, U.S.A. (priv. coll.)*

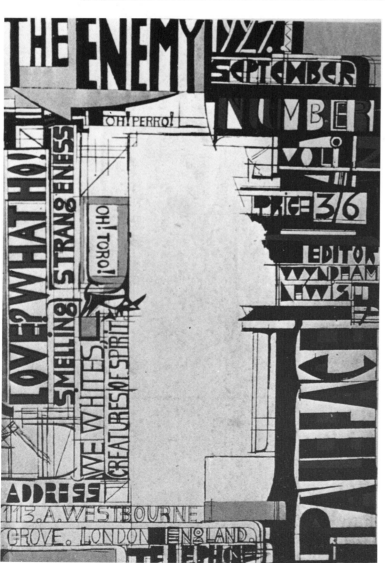

WYNDHAM LEWIS, The Enemy *magazine cover, September 1927, Great Britain (priv. coll.)*

WYNDHAM LEWIS, Blast *magazine cover, July 1915, Great Britain (priv. coll.)*

Commercial Design

The tendency of today is toward new forms, new rhythms, to break sharply from tradition and go forth freshly to a newer and untried world.

This quotation, from a 1927 advertisement illustrated by Marie Laurencin, epitomized the bold spirit of the graphic artist in the early twentieth century, when Art Deco's extraordinary vitality was at its peak. Its revolutionary principles of design produced a breakthrough in graphics that gave birth to commercial design as a recognized profession and the graphic artist as its practitioner. Modern design spawned a universal new graphic language that redefined layout, typography, and presentation in commercial applications. This was a unique time, when commercial advertising, product design, and marketing came into their own and established an enduring business-artist bond.

The cultural climate

Although the rebellious thrust of modernism in the fine arts affected commercial design—freeing it by such experiments as the use of free-floating type by Dadaists and Futurists and the highly organized geometric layouts of Cubists and Constructivists—those influences were not strongly evident until the 1920s. The roots of the new graphics actually go back further, to the turn of the century, when certain artists from Austria, Scotland, and Germany rejected the curves and complexities of Art Nouveau in favor of simplicity, linearity, and unifying art with the period's exciting new technology.

At Art Deco's peak, a sweeping new criterion was established: all products must be viewed from an aesthetic standpoint; form must enhance function. An explosion of new products brought a commensurate outpouring of product designs and advertising to promote them. Being stylish in the 1920s (as in the high-tech 1980s) meant owning the latest, most highly designed products available. Industrial design was born from the desire to make products not only efficient but beautiful.

Graphic designers created trademarks, labels, and packages. Carl Otto Czeschka's elegant L. Wolff cigar label* was one of more than twenty printed about 1915 for this Hamburg company. The labels were red and white, with geometric gold foil decoration printed in relief. Cosmetics and perfumes were frequently packaged in the Art Deco style. In the early 1930s Ayao Yamana and Mitsugu Maeda produced striking designs for Shiseido in Japan. Yamana's face-powder box of 1932 shows both fashion and avant-garde tendencies. (In many Japanese designs of the period illustrations showed a Western rather than Asian woman, perhaps to maintain the Deco look.)

Specialization was not as prevalent in the Deco era as it became later. A graphic artist might design matchboxes one day, posters the next, and textiles the day after. George Barbier, perhaps best known for his *haute couture*

187

ANONYMOUS, *"Bourgognes Rouges," menu, c. 1925, France (priv. coll.)*

AYAO YAMANA, *"Shiseido Modern Colour Face Powder," package, 1932, Japan (Shiseido Cosmetics, Japan)*

fashion illustrations and theatrical sets and costumes, also produced posters, advertisements, magazine covers, boxes, book illustrations, and wallpaper. Other artists whose designs ranged from jewelry to furniture and brochures were Charles Martin, Charles Gesmar, Erté, Georges Lepape, Bakst, Zig, Iribe, Marty, and Brunelleschi. Iribe was one of the most versatile. His cover for the brochure *Catastrophe* was one of many he designed for the wine merchant Nicolas. He also designed jewelry for Chanel, sets for Hollywood extravaganzas, textiles, and furniture. He produced fashion illustrations and political caricatures and somehow made time to found and edit several magazines and newspapers.

Germany: the marriage of art and industry

For most of the nineteenth century there was little formal or organized graphic design activity. Graphic artists tended to work individually and on a small scale. In the 1890s, with the development of color lithography, there was a burst of activity in magazine graphics and posters that stimulated interest by important artists of the time—including painters like Bonnard and Toulouse-Lautrec.

German architect-designer Peter Behrens was pivotal in the development of modern commercial design. Along with other avant-garde architects at the turn of the century—notably Mackintosh in Glasgow and Hoffmann in Vienna—Behrens sought to reconcile art with industry and give commercial products and architectural interiors serious aesthetic consideration. In 1900, nearly two decades before the Bauhaus, he designed a pioneering book, *Feste des Lebens*, set entirely in sans-serif type. Behrens became director of the Düsseldorf School of Arts and Crafts in 1903. Four years later he was named design director of the A.E.G. (Allgemeine Elektricitäts-Gesellschaft), one of the world's largest electrical-equipment manufacturers. There he was able to put his advanced ideas into practice (as evidenced by his unique poster

22 "A.E.G. Metallfadenlampe"*) and created the first major corporate design program. This work won him recognition as the world's first industrial designer. Behrens then became the primary force behind the Deutsche Werkbund, precursor of the Bauhaus, both of which aspired to create a unity among architect, artist, and artisan and to elevate the functional and aesthetic values of mass production. He influenced a generation of artists and architects (among them Walter Gropius, Mies van der Rohe, and Le Corbusier) who were to provide the foundations for the graphic arts of the twentieth century.

Lucien Bernhard was the first important graphic artist to emerge from Behrens's teachings. His posters and other commercial graphics, typically using little more than a logo and an image of a product, were the epitome of simplicity, and many were early examples of Art Deco style. Bernhard's success was immediate. When he entered his first poster for Priester matches in a 1903 contest, the judges thought it too revolutionary and eliminated it from the competition. Ernst Growald, a printer, literally retrieved it from a wastebasket and then persuaded the committee of Bernhard's genius. Bernhard won first prize. He went on to study architecture and built a number of outstanding houses and factories. He also designed wallpaper, furniture, objets d'art, over three hundred product packages, and more than

171 thirty typefaces. Bernhard's advertisement for the Audi automobile in 1920,* which preceded Cassandre's first poster, "Au Bûcheron," by three years,

PAUL IRIBE, *"Catastrophe,"* brochure for Nicolas Wine Merchants, c. 1930, France (D. De Lattre, Paris)

158

A. HILDEBRANDT, *"Hörch,"* advertisement, 1920, Germany (priv. coll.)

LUCIEN BERNHARD, *"Priester"* (matches), poster, 1903, Germany shows his allegiance to simple illustration, typography, and layout, as well as his energetic promotion of modernity. The three-dimensional-appearing logo device was adopted in German, French, and American advertisements to convey the idea of Futurism and speed.

Germany had an impressive number of other talented graphic artists, such as Ludwig Hohlwein, Walter Schnackenberg, Julius Gipkins, Julius Klinger (originally from Austria), Ernst Deutsch, and Hans Rudi Erdt, who helped lay the foundations of twentieth-century graphic design. While not all of their work was styled in the Art Deco manner, much of it reflected the German inclination toward modernism. Gipkins in particular was prolific in advertising design and packaging. His packages for the Italian candy manufacturer Sarotti* were some of the boldest designs of the time.

189

Influence of the Bauhaus

48

Considering the seeds sown in Germany, it is easy to understand the formation in 1919 of the Bauhaus—a collective of architects, artists, and designers dedicated to developing a style of design in architecture and applied arts that would wed form to function. The Bauhaus crystallized the new graphic concepts; it was to become the single most important influence in twentieth-century design. Some of the most prominent artists of the time—Feininger,* Kandinsky, Klee, and Moholy-Nagy, to mention a few—worked on graphics as well as other Bauhaus activities. Although initially advertising design was not taught at the Bauhaus, it became a major subject, along with poster art and printing. The Bauhaus was strongly involved in wallpaper and textile design, and many designs were produced commercially for German firms. In addition, the Bauhaus designed promotion and sales displays, and some were mass-produced as early as 1924.

When Moholy-Nagy, who had a passion for typography, took over the printing workshop in 1923, he developed the basic principles of modern graphic design. These ideas were eagerly absorbed into the Art Deco style and became powerful tools in the design of advertising. Designs created with the technique attracted the viewer's attention through bold provocation and distortion, and held it by forcing the eye to explore extraordinary images. Moholy-Nagy's disciple, the Austrian-born Herbert Bayer, took over from 1925 to 1928 and extended his predecessor's innovations. During that period, Joost Schmidt introduced the first course in lettering. Schmidt took the helm in 1928, when the printing workshop was renamed the Commercial Art Department—and in 1928 the very idea of "commercial art" was a revolutionary concept.

Bayer, only twenty-five when he took over the printing workshop, eventually became one of the most important commercial art figures of our time. At the Bauhaus he formulated theories governing advertising, layout, and typography. From 1928 to 1938 he worked in Berlin as a typographer, painter, photographer, exhibition designer, director of an advertising agency, and art director for the German edition of *Vogue* magazine. Bayer then moved to the United States to become a design consultant for *Fortune* magazine. He also worked for major advertising agencies, including J. Walter Thompson.

Other important artists were influenced by the Bauhaus program. At age twenty-one, Jan Tschichold saw the first comprehensive Bauhaus exhibition

ADDIATOR

Above, left to right
KARL SCHULPIG, *trademark for Addiator, Germany*
OTTO WOLF, *trademark for himself, Germany*
ZERO, *trademark for Julius Runge, Germany*

WASSILY KANDINSKY, *"Bauhaus-Ausstellung," postcard no. 3, 1923, Germany (Bauhaus-Archiv Museum für Gestaltung, Berlin)*

PAUL KLEE, *"Bauhaus-Ausstellung," postcard no. 4, 1923, Germany (Bauhaus-Archiv Museum für Gestaltung, Berlin)*

in 1923, and as a result combined Constructivist and Bauhaus concepts to create (from 1926 to 1929) a "universal" alphabet, one of the most influential German contributions to typography. He was hailed as a major force in graphics,* but soon, in the Nazi era, his work was denounced and halted. In 1933 he was arrested, charged with having created an "un-German" typography. Six weeks later he was released, and soon after he emigrated to Switzerland, where he worked primarily as a book designer.

28,29

The French influence

France made its main contribution to modern commercial design in the early years of the Deco era, most notably in posters. Generally, the French graphic style was less theoretical and revolutionary than the German. France made a transition from Art Nouveau to Art Deco, streamlining Art Nouveau and modernizing it with a characteristic Gallic flair for gaiety and decoration. Major artists made significant advances in posters and advertisements, from Chéret and Toulouse-Lautrec to the "Musketeers": Cassandre, Carlu, Loupot, and Colin.

With so much avant-garde activity in painting and sculpture from 1900 to 1925, it was inevitable that these revolutionary ideas would spill over to the applied arts. French graphic artists used the art movements to harmonize their designs and strengthen their compositions with eye-catching devices and symbols. Commercial design in France was not the organized, serious study it was in Germany—instead, it was highly individualized—but it was just as important in taking the graphic arts to a new level of excellence.

Graphic design in Belgium, Switzerland, and Italy

In Belgium, the two most important figures were René Magritte and Léo Marfurt. Following World War I, Magritte designed wallpaper, fashion illustrations, posters, and striking sheet music covers in the Art Deco style. "Arlite,"* a sheet music cover, is the epitome of Art Deco, its basic components simplicity, geometricism, distortion, and repetition. Marfurt, who worked out of his own advertising and design studio, Les Créations Publicitaires, created some of the most cubistic Art Deco posters.*

219

72, 307

Ernst Keller, who produced magnificent Deco posters in his native Switzerland, was a major force in graphic design. Beginning in 1918, he taught advertising and layout for more than forty years at the Zurich School of Applied Art, where he created the first Swiss professional program in typography and design. Swiss designer Herbert Matter gained international acclaim for his pioneering work in developing photomontage. In Austria, Joseph Binder stood out as the most important Deco designer until the early thirties, when he went to the United States and extended his already major reputation.

Italian artists tended to work in an informal, unstructured way; their Deco graphics derived primarily from the popular French styles. Perhaps Italy's most important figure in the move toward modern commercial design was the architect and designer Gio Ponti. He founded Italy's major interior decoration magazines, *Domus* (1929) and *Lo Stile* (1941); in 1933 he organized the trendsetting Milan Triennale. Ponti influenced his contemporaries to create clean, uncluttered works in the modern style. The Ricordi printing company, which commissioned modern artists for its advertising campaigns, produced

ANONYMOUS, *"Exposition Internationale, Paris," brochure, 1937, France (D. De Lattre, Paris)*

REMOSO, *"USTQ Fête Annuelle," program, February 1931, France (Musée des Arts Décoratifs, Paris)*

some of the best graphics of the period, including postcards, advertisements, and posters. Italy's postcard designs were outstanding. The most prolific artist was Giovanni Nanni, who created postcards for the F. Polenghi firm in Torino; his stylish elongated women often were accompanied by the sleek, elegant borzoi dog.

Great Britain and modernist design

Great Britain was generally resistant to modern commercial design. In 1907, for instance, a proposal to erect outdoor advertising billboards was met with a public outcry that resulted in an official act making it an offense to "disfigure the natural beauty of the landscape." As late as 1930, Englishman Frank Young, in his book *Modern Advertising Art*, wrote that modernism "is still in its infancy here." More scathing is this 1929 review of English advertising practices by C. Harold Vernon, an advertising agency owner:

> In England we are forced to await novelty in importations from abroad, while those who cannot be bothered with design are well content to have their advertisements set, as Oscar Wilde wrote in another context, in "one of those typical English faces, once seen never remembered." Germany and France contribute the best of our new types—simply because artists and designers in these countries are closely allied with the printing craft. In England they are still very much cold-shouldered. But there are many, inside and outside of advertising, who have a deeprooted prejudice against this forward movement as a whole. "Modern" advertising to them is synonymous with "jazz" and "stunt" or, a really whole-hearted condemnation, "German." They [the English] are the "sell the goods" and "get down to brass tacks" school; they are the sound businessmen whose enterprise and verve have contributed so much to the present flourishing condition of British industries, and who can, of course, afford to sneer at the contemptible little successes attained by the revolutionary Germans and the "scrap and rebuild" Americans.
>
> I fear that the truth is that our British industries are sadly missing a generation wiped out by the war. The younger generation is only just beginning to make its influence felt at the sleepy conferences of the Old Business.

GIOVANNI NANNI, *"Bonne Année," postcard, c. 1915, Italy (coll. Iris Hoffman)*

161

The one important English force for modernism behind the scenes at this time was Frank Pick, art director of London Transport advertising, who was responsible for obtaining the most stylish and modern graphics in England. The unsigned "Olympia Motor Show" poster was one of many outstanding London Transport designs. It was produced in a small size (approximately 18×24″) and used for window display and point-of-purchase selling. Of somewhat less consequence to Art Deco graphics was Eric Gill, who created
29 some important modern type designs (such as Gill Sans*) and advocated the use of unjustified (flush-left lines of uneven length) typesetting—which he used in setting the text of his 1931 book *Typography*—but, for all his pioneering, retained a strong tie to tradition. Other English graphic artists worth
284 noting were Tom Purvis, Austin Cooper,* and P. M. Batty.

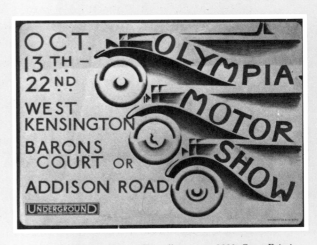

ANONYMOUS, *"Olympia Motor Show," poster, c. 1930, Great Britain (coll. Roger Coisman)*

Eastern Europe

The countries of Eastern Europe had some excellent commercial designers, but no Deco graphics movement as such. The Hungarian Csabai-Ekes was known for his packages and magazine advertisements. Promoting such products as perfume and candy, Csabai-Ekes combined a geometric and folk art touch, as in "Floris," with female images as sleek and stylized as any in France. His "Femina Kalapszalon" (1929) shows the influence of Cubism in its sharp angles. The lower half of the design is a clever abstraction revealing only a hint of the woman's breast and her string of pearls. In Poland there was Tadeus Gronowski; Russia gave us Cassandre, Alexey Brodovitch, and Mehemed Agha (all of whom moved to Paris and then New York); and Czech artists included Hlaváčk,* Otokar Makvicka, Vit Obrtel, Karel Teige,* and Jindrich Styrsky.

243/46, 246, 251

162

CSABAI-EKES, *"Femina Kalapszalon," advertisement, 1929, Hungary (priv. coll.)*

Commercial graphics in America

The American involvement in Art Deco was late and scanty compared to the feverish activity in France and Germany before 1925. In the 1910s and early '20s, *Vogue* and *Vanity Fair* magazines adapted their cover designs to European styles, importing graphics mainly from France. It wasn't until the mid-twenties that America really woke up to the Deco style; in fact, the United States did not participate in the 1925 Paris Exposition. By 1928 scores of ad campaigns showed the influence of modernism, including those for Lord & Taylor, Marshall Field, Bamberger's, Union Pacific, Fisher Body, Saks, Nash "400," Texaco, Victrola, and Macy's, and perfumers such as Houbigant, Roget & Gallet, Caron, and Coty. Still, the basic design ideas were imported from Europe, although Henry Clive, W. J. Benda, William Welsh, and Frank McIntosh made important commercial advertising design contributions.

Instead, something quite different was fermenting in the United States: advertising as an industry was coming of age. Mass marketing was being developed to accommodate a country that stretched three thousand miles coast to coast. Magazines were mobilized by businesses working through market-wise advertising agencies. Enormous sums of money were spent on these campaigns, and more was spent to develop irresistible product designs. Advertisers now focused on consumer psychology. The J. Walter Thompson Company, for example, took the general antiseptic Listerine from approximately $100,000 in sales in 1920 to over $4,000,000 in 1927 by promoting it as a mouthwash, a cure for dandruff, an after-shave, a cure for colds and sore throats, a deodorant, and an astringent. American advertising was thus responsible for a marketing revolution that included total product design, consumer analysis, and massive advertising campaigns.

During this period, political instability in Europe caused many Deco artists to seek refuge in America. Perhaps more important, the magazine industry, which had grown steadily during the 1920s—especially the numerous women's and entertainment publications—now exploded with advertisements as a result of the new marketing techniques. This meant lucrative work for the graphic artists who chose to live in America. With the important contributions of the forward-thinking Russian art directors of *Vogue* and *Harper's Bazaar*—Agha and Brodovitch, respectively—the thirties in America produced some of the finest modern graphics seen anywhere.

There was a great deal of experimentation in the 1930s. Layouts used asymmetrical designs, juxtaposed seemingly disparate typographical elements, and presented unexpected contrasts. One of the most advanced graphic design programs of any American business was that of Container Corporation of America, whose president, Walter P. Paepke, commissioned outstanding designers like Cassandre, Léger, Man Ray, Matter, and Carlu for the company's institutional advertising campaigns. (Paepke was an important supporter of the efforts of Moholy-Nagy and Gropius to continue the teachings of the Bauhaus in the United States.) But as advertising agencies mushroomed in America, their effect on the artist was a mixed blessing. Although illustrators had a lot of work and made sizable fees, inevitably the quality of their work was affected. Illustrators were forced to bend to the will of advertisers, to follow the fads of public taste, and to reflect the new mass-psychology marketing concepts. An artist who didn't change his style or technique to conform to current advertising practices ran the risk of being considered resistant or, even worse, dated. Many gifted graphic designers were caught in this trap during the 1930s. Further, advertising was moving tentatively toward photography. Some of the early commercial photographers used Deco illustration devices in their layouts—for example, the Hungarian-born Martin Munkacsi angled his camera to give images the thrusting diagonals so often employed by Deco artists to signify speed and power—but eventually photography, propelled by the publication of *Life* in 1936, was to undercut the Art Deco style.

In editorial illustration Art Deco, which depended on distorting or transforming reality, could not coexist with photojournalism, which captured people and events realistically. The domination of photography extended into all areas of commercial design until the 1970 revival of Art Deco, when it once more was to share its place with imaginative Deco-style illustration.

A. M. CASSANDRE, *"Dole Pineapple Juice," advertisement, 1938, U.S.A. (priv. coll.)*

ADVERTISING

Each country projected its own style in the advertising of the Art Deco period. Japan's designs often had a lightness in color or a spaciousness of layout not evident in the designs of other countries. French advertisements were usually intellectual conceptions stemming from the avant-garde movements, such as Alexey Brodovitch's "Aux Trois Quartiers"* and "Madelios"* designs, made for department stores in Paris, which showed the influence of Cubism and Constructivism. The French designers also used Futurist elements, with an emphasis on speed. German advertisements were often powerful and emotional, reflecting that country's passion for Expressionism, while at the same time incorporating Cubist and Futurist characteristics. For instance, in Ludwig Hohlwein's "Tachometerwerke"* and Müller-Kludt's "Farbenfabriken Otto Baer"* the facial expressions are extraordinarily determined and quite unlike those of countries where gaiety prevailed. The dominant approach of American Art Deco artists was that of cuteness, reflecting the popular interest in flappers in the so-called roaring twenties. However, European émigrés of the 1930s, with their often intellectual approach and highly stylized designs, brought substance to American advertising design.

177
178, 180
186
167

GEORGES FAVRE, "Berger-Grillon," advertising sign and poster, 1930, France (Pat Kery Fine Arts, New York)

ANONYMOUS, *"Nicolas Wine Merchant," brochure cover, c. 1930, France (priv. coll.)*

VILMOS HUSZAR, *"Van Nelle's Thee," advertisements, 1924, The Netherlands (John Vloemans Antiquarian Books, The Hague)*

ATELIERS ALBANS, *"Fly-Tox," advertisement, c. 1935, France (priv. coll.)*

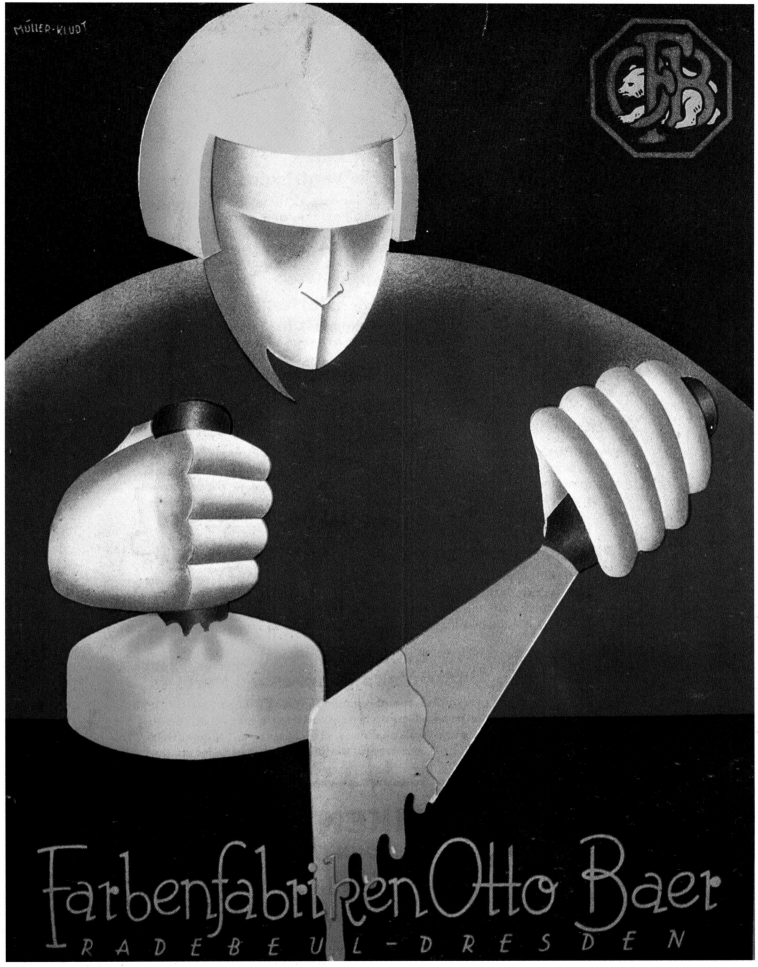

MÜLLER-KLUDT, *"Farbenfabriken Otto Baer," advertisement, c. 1930, Germany (priv. coll.)*

CHARLES LOUPOT, *"St. Raphaël Quinquina," advertising sign and poster, c. 1945, France (Pat Kery Fine Arts, New York)*

A. M. CASSANDRE, *"Casino," advertising sign, c. 1930, France (Marcel Fleiss Galerie 1900–2000, Paris)*

FRANZ BILKO, *"China-Tee," department store advertising project, c. 1920, Austria (Hochschule für Angewandte Kunst, Vienna)*

F. E. NEUMANN, *"GDA," advertisement, 1920, Germany (priv. coll.)*

LUCIEN BERNHARD, *"Audi," advertisement, 1920, Germany (priv. coll.)*

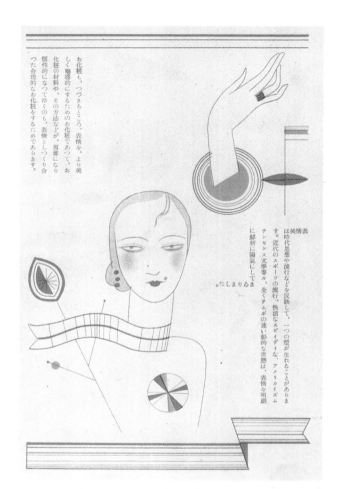

AYAO YAMANA, *advertisement, 1930, Japan (Shiseido Cosmetics, Tokyo)*

EDMUND EDEL, *"Die Weite Welt," advertisement and poster, 1900, Germany (priv. coll.)*

PAUL IRIBE, *"Je n'entends pas ce que je bois," Nicolas Wine Merchant brochure, c. 1930, France (D. De Lattre, Paris)*

LONGLEY, *"Underground," window sign, c. 1930, Great Britain (coll. Roger Coisman)*

HERBERT BAYER, *"der neue Adler" (automobile), prospectus, 1929,
Germany*

GUSTAV TENGGREN, *"Blue Moon Silk Stockings," advertisement,
1926, U.S.A. (priv. coll.)*

GEORGES MASSIOT, *"Porto Sandeman," advertisement and poster,
c. 1931, France (Nicholas Bailly, New York)*

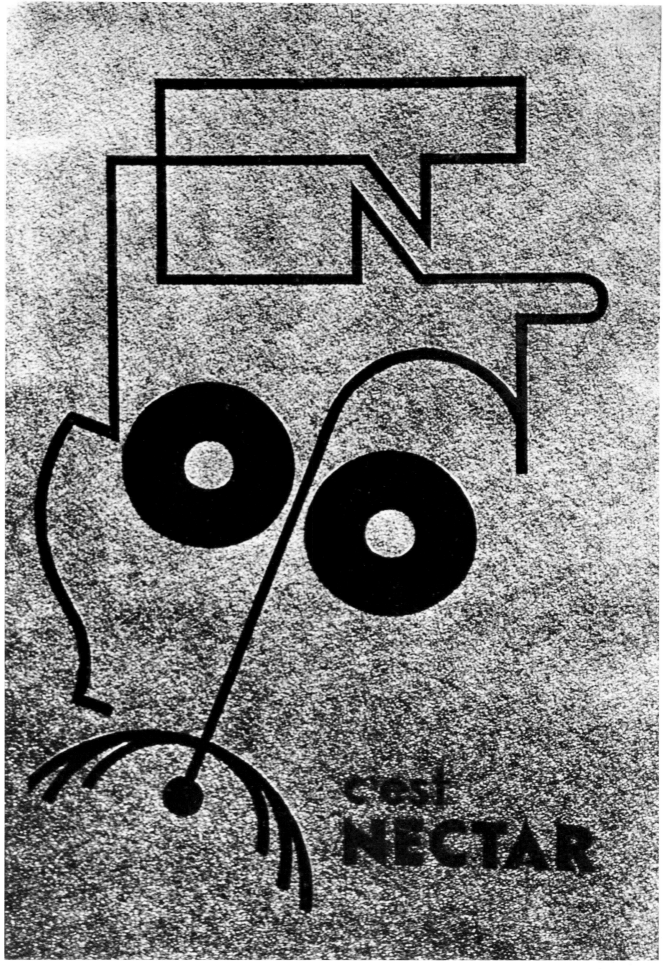

A. M. CASSANDRE, *"C'est nectar," Nicolas Wine Merchant brochure, 1930, France (D. De Lattre, Paris)*

RENÉ MAGRITTE, "Alfa Romeo," advertisement, 1925, Belgium (coll. Brigitte Homburg)

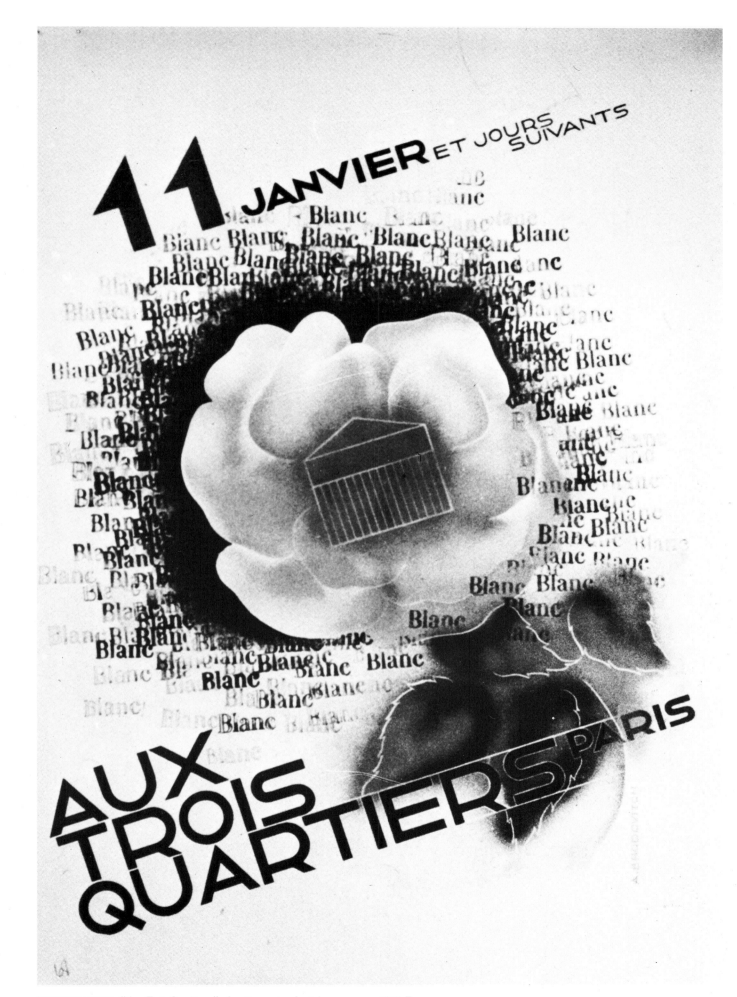

ALEXEY BRODOVITCH, *"Aux Trois Quartiers," advertisement and catalogue cover, c. 1930, France (priv. coll.)*

LÉON BENIGNI, *"Le Coupé Sport," brochure illustration, 1930, France (Bibliothèque Forney, Paris)*

LEONETTO CAPPIELLO, *"Parapluie-Revel," leaflet and poster, 1922, France (Nicholas Bailly, New York)*

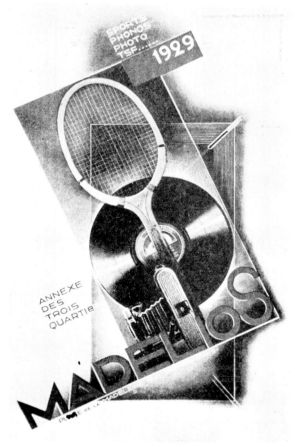

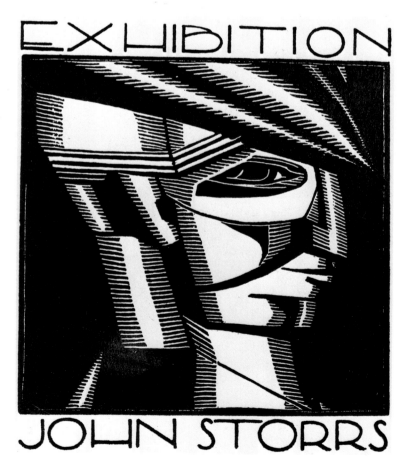

ALEXEY BRODOVITCH, *"Madelios," catalogue cover, 1929, France (priv. coll.)*

JOHN STORRS, *"Exhibition John Storrs," catalogue cover, 1920, U.S.A. (from the Mitchell C. Wolfson Jr. Collection of Decorative and Propaganda Arts, Miami)*

A. M. CASSANDRE, *Dubonnet advertisement and poster, 1935, France (Pat Kery Fine Arts, New York)*

ALEXEY BRODOVITCH, *"Madelios," advertisement and poster, 1928, France (Pat Kery Fine Arts, New York)*

JEAN CARLU, *"Au Bon Marché," advertisement and poster, 1932, France (priv. coll.)*

ANONYMOUS, *"Candee," advertisement and poster, 1929, Switzerland (Musée des Arts Décoratifs, Paris)*

ANONYMOUS, *"Nicolas Wine Merchant," brochure cover, c. 1930, France (D. De Lattre, Paris)*

BOULNOIRES, "*Bandit de Robert Piguet,*" advertisement, c. 1935, France-U.S.A. (priv. coll.)

MARCEL VERTÈS, "*Shocking de Schiaparelli,*" advertisement, c. 1935, U.S.A. (coll. Michael Schler)

CIGARETTES
BELGA

LÉO MARFURT, *"Belga Cigarettes," advertising sign and poster, c. 1930, Belgium (priv. coll.)*

LUDWIG HOHLWEIN, *"Tachometerwerke," advertisement, 1920, Germany (priv. coll.)*

PACKAGING

By the 1920s the European tradition of handcrafted packaging had moved into mass production, although some companies still used high-quality printing methods, such as lithographic or stenciled pochoir prints.

The cosmetics industry was particularly active in creating handsome packaging to promote the image of the modern woman. During the 1920s and '30s, the Shiseido cosmetics company in Japan created a multitude of high-quality 221 Art Deco–style graphics for its packages, including labels for matchboxes* that were given away in the company's ice-cream parlor in the Ginza area of Tokyo.

In the 1920s it became fashionable for women to smoke, and modern graphics often showed women playfully or elegantly holding cigarettes or surrounded by a romantic haze of smoke. In their packaging, tobacco companies exploited the latest fads, such as the passion for anything Egyptian or Turkish that followed the exotic productions of the Ballets Russes. As cigarette lines were expanded, packaging became increasingly important. Various brands were packaged with designs emphasizing the modern obsessions: sunshine, health, riches, leisure, automobiles, elegant restaurants, and luxury travel.

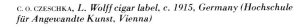

C. O. CZESCHKA, *L. Wolff cigar label, c. 1915, Germany (Hochschule für Angewandte Kunst, Vienna)*

M. PONTY, *Gitanes cigarette box, 1930, France (coll. Nicholas Bailly)*

ANONYMOUS, *"Sérénade de Fleurs," Rimmel Perfumeries, perfume label, 1925, France (Bibliothèque Forney, Paris)*

JULIUS GIPKINS, *"Sarotti Citronen Schnitte," candy package, 1920,
Germany (priv. coll.)*

RECO CAPEY, *"Yardley's April Violets," perfume package, 1929, Great Britain (priv. coll.)*

ANONYMOUS, *"L'Heure de Rimmel," perfume label, 1925, France (Bibliothèque Forney, Paris)*

ANONYMOUS, *"Savon de Toilette aux Fleurs," Kramp & Co.,*
package, 1921, Germany (priv. coll.)

ANONYMOUS, *"Marta à la Corbeille Royale,"* face powder box, c. 1920,
France (priv. coll.)

WALTER KAMPMANN, *"Parfumerie Elberfeld Morisse,"* box covering
paper, 1920, Germany (priv. coll.)

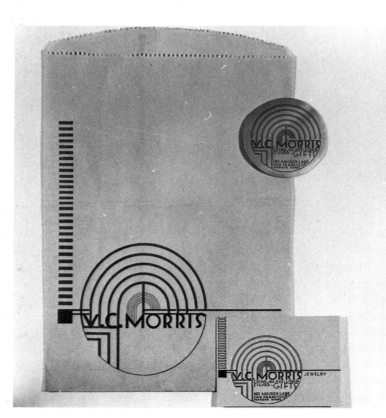

FRANK LLOYD WRIGHT, *"V. C. Morris Store,"* adhesive seal and small
shopping bag, c. 1942, U.S.A. (from the Mitchell C. Wolfson Jr.
Collection of Decorative and Propaganda Arts, Miami)

CORRESPONDENCE

In any era, the styles of correspondence play a meaningful part in personal, social, and business communication. The 1920s and '30s saw a particularly rich outpouring of innovative graphic designs in stationery, letterheads, invitations, and postcards, many of which reflected Art Deco style.

Stationery, perceived as an extension of the self, was never more richly conceived than by Gaut-Blancan et Cie. of Paris, who engaged some of the best artists of the day to create (often anonymously) imaginative designs that
193 –197   were gorgeously printed by silk-screen on handsome colored papers.*

Postcards were enormously popular by the turn of the century. First introduced in 1869, they were an instant success in both Europe and America. In the 1890s the new lithographic process enabled inexpensive yet high-quality mass reproduction. Encouraged by this technological development, a number of leading poster artists turned to postcards as another opportunity to present their work to the public. According to posterist Leonetto Cappiello, the postcard was "a very useful tool to reveal art to the masses." Two decades later, postcards were as popular as ever, and even some of the Bauhaus artists worked in this medium. Feininger, Klee, Kandinsky, and Bayer produced
159   postcards* for the important 1923 exhibition celebrating the first four years of the Bauhaus. Bayer was the strongest in the Deco style; his most memorable
28   postcard* showed a splendid geometric face outlined in black and white, designed by Oskar Schlemmer, which was later to appear on the Bauhaus seal. It was common practice for posters to be reduced for postcards, such as
204   Cassandre's 1931 "Triplex" poster,* originally an ad for automobile safety glass.

Invitations were another form of correspondence embraced creatively by the Deco movement, particularly in France. In the 1920s and '30s, as in the previous generation, the artists' ball of the Beaux Arts School in Paris was one of the most bizarre events of the year. It included a procession of artists from Montmartre to the school on the Left Bank (in the 1890s, Toulouse-Lautrec and his circle were among the annual participants), sometimes with artists' models marching naked. In the Deco period, one American woman attending rode bare-breasted on an elephant, accompanied by her husband, who carried a bag of live snakes and wore a neckpiece of dead pigeons. The invitations to these balls were appropriately risqué, as the "4 Z'Arts" (*Quatres*
199   *Arts*)* design of 1928 demonstrates.

ANONYMOUS, *"Arlequin," Gaut-Blancan et Cie. stationery design, 1924–30, France (Bibliothèque Forney, Paris)*

ANONYMOUS, *"Frimas," Gaut-Blancan et Cie. stationery design, 1924–30, France (Bibliothèque Forney, Paris)*

ANONYMOUS, *"Fleurs Nouvelles," Gaut-Blancan et Cie. stationery design, 1924–30, France (Bibliothèque Forney, Paris)*

ANONYMOUS, *"Stella," Gaut-Blancan et Cie. stationery design, 1924–30, France (Bibliothèque Forney, Paris)*

ANONYMOUS, *"Ma Jolie," Gaut-Blancan et Cie. stationery design, 1924–30, France (Bibliothèque Forney, Paris)*

ANONYMOUS, *"Modern," Gaut-Blancan et Cie. stationery design, 1924–30, France (Bibliothèque Forney, Paris)*

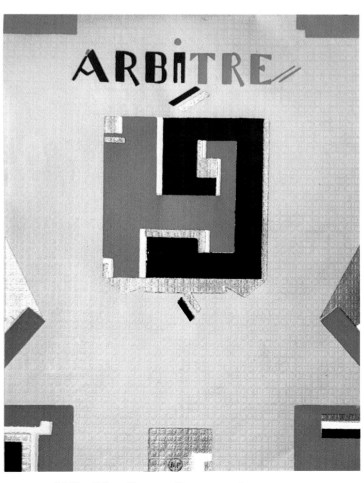

ANONYMOUS, *"Arbitre," Gaut-Blancan et Cie. stationery design, 1924–30, France (Bibliothèque Forney, Paris)*

ANONYMOUS, *"Isca," Gaut-Blancan et Cie. stationery design,*
1924–30, France (Bibliothèque Forney, Paris)

ANONYMOUS, *"Festival," Gaut-Blancan et Cie. stationery design,*
1924–30, France (Bibliothèque Forney, Paris)

ANONYMOUS, *"Rialto," Gaut-Blancan et Cie. stationery design,*
1924–30, France (Bibliothèque Forney, Paris)

ANONYMOUS, *"Paris," Gaut-Blancan et Cie. stationery design, 1924–30, France (Bibliothèque Forney, Paris)*

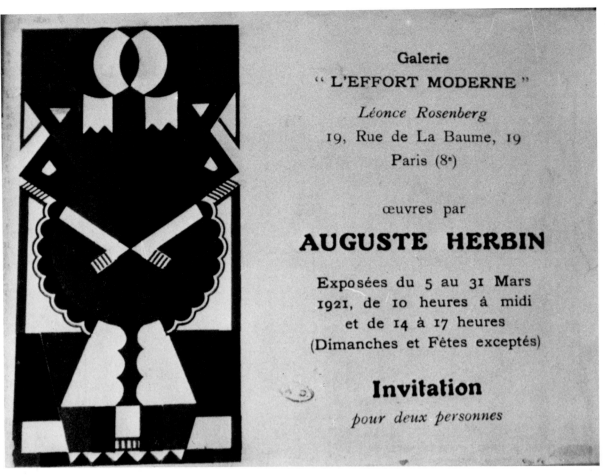

AUGUSTE HERBIN, *"Galerie L'Effort Moderne," exhibition invitation, 1921, France (Musée des Arts Décoratifs, Paris)*

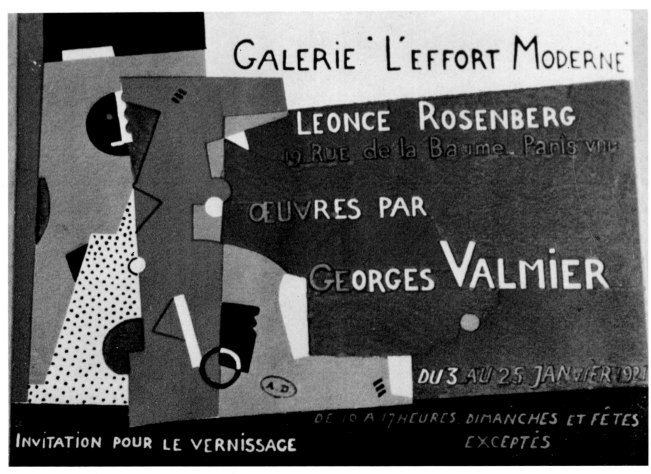

GEORGES VALMIER, *"Galerie L'Effort Moderne," exhibition invitation, 1921, France (Musée des Arts Décoratifs, Paris)*

ANONYMOUS, *"Bal de L'Internat," invitation, 1930, France (Musée des Arts Décoratifs, Paris)*

199

SERGE SOCATOFF, *"4 Z'Arts," invitation, 1928, France (Musée des Arts Décoratifs, Paris)*

ANONYMOUS, *untitled, postcard, 1935, Japan (Shiseido Cosmetics, Tokyo)*

VITTORIO ZEICHIN, *"Zenit," postcard, c. 1908, Italy (coll. Iris Hoffman)*

ANONYMOUS, *untitled, postcard, c. 1935, U.S.A. (coll. Iris Hoffman)*

Établissements Delac, Vandal & Cie

SALLE MARIVAUX

Mardi 15 Avril 191

ANDRÉ MARTY, *"Salle Mari Vaux,"* invitation, 1919, France (Musée des Arts Décoratifs, Paris)

204

ANONYMOUS, *untitled, postcard, 1935, Japan (Shiseido Cosmetics, Tokyo)*

A. M. CASSANDRE, *"Triplex" (safety glass), postcard based on poster, 1931, France (Jacques Mallet Fine Arts, New York*

EX·ALTO·AD·SIGNUM·

ANONYMOUS, *"Ex Alto Ad Signum," postcard, c. 1930, Italy (coll. Iris Hoffman)*

BENTI-VEGLIO, *untitled, postcard, c. 1925, Italy (coll. Iris Hoffman)*

WALLPAPER & TEXTILES

In the Art Deco period, it seems, almost everyone in the arts became involved in creating printed designs for wallpaper and textiles. Included were painters such as Sonia Delaunay, Raoul Dufy, and the Russians Alexandra Exter, Kasimir Malevich, and Varvara Stepanova. Paul Klee designed textiles at the Bauhaus, and in Vienna, Secessionist and Wiener Werkstätte founders Koloman Moser and Josef Hoffmann created bold geometric textile designs as early as the 1890s.

Illustrators and cartoonists also did textile designs, including Herman-Paul, a German caricaturist for *Simplicissimus*; Iribe, the French founder and caricaturist-illustrator of the publications *Le Témoin* and *Le Mot*; English book illustrator Paul Nash; McKnight-Kauffer, the American graphic artist working in Great Britain; and, working in the United States, Ilonka Karasz, *New Yorker* cover artist; Antonio Petrucelli, *Fortune* cover artist; and avant-garde photographer Edward Steichen. Many artists known for fashion and costume design were also involved in this field, including Erté, Marty, Lepape, Barbier, and Martin.

Of the painters, the most active designer of textiles was Sonia Delaunay, 216 whose "simultané" fabrics* were inspired by Simultanism, the art movement dealing with the effects of color, which she cofounded in 1912 with her husband, Robert. Born in the Ukraine, Sonia Delaunay had a dramatic sense of color, derived in part from childhood memories of Russian folk art. Her fabric designs had a strong impact on the world of fashion and interior decoration, and she was one of the founders of Op Art. Indeed, a garment 287 made of one of her fabrics (shown on a *Vogue* magazine cover* of 1924) was called the "optical" dress.

VARVARA STEPANOVA, *untitled, textile design, 1920, Russia*

C.-G. DUFRESNE, *untitled, textile design, c. 1925, France (Musée des Arts Décoratifs, Paris)*

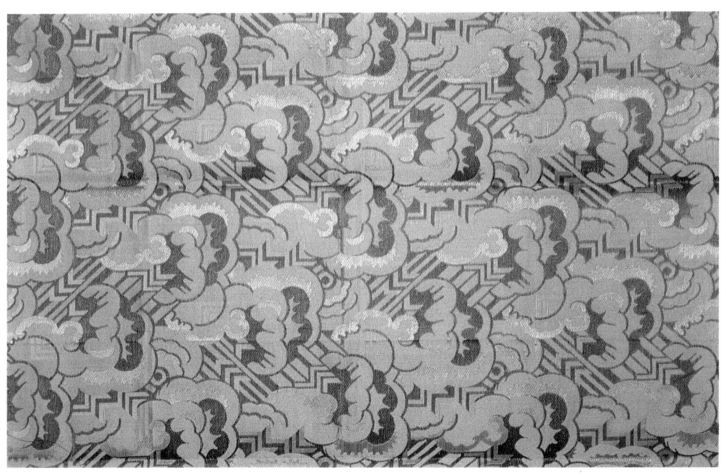

BOUDART, *untitled, textile design, 1925–30, France (Musée des Arts Décoratifs, Paris)*

ANONYMOUS, *"Français," Leroy Co. wallpaper design, 1930, France (Bibliothèque Forney, Paris)*

ANONYMOUS, *Leroy Co. wallpaper design, c. 1925, France
(Bibliothèque Forney, Paris)*

RAOUL DUFY, *"La Mousson," textile design, 1925, France (Musée des Arts Décoratifs, Paris)*

JOSEF HOFFMANN, *textile design, Wiener Werkstätte, c. 1908, Austria (Hochschule für Angewandte Kunst, Vienna)*

ANONYMOUS, *Leroy Co. wallpaper design, c. 1925, France*
(Bibliothèque Forney, Paris)

ATELIER MARTINE, *Desfosse & Karth wallpaper design, c. 1927,*
France (Bibliothèque Forney, Paris)

ANONYMOUS, *Leroy Co. wallpaper design, c. 1925, France (Bibliothèque Forney, Paris)*

E.-A. SEGUY, *Leroy Co. wallpaper design, 1925, France (Bibliothèque Forney, Paris)*

213

ANONYMOUS, *Leroy Co. wallpaper design, c. 1925, France (Bibliothèque Forney, Paris)*

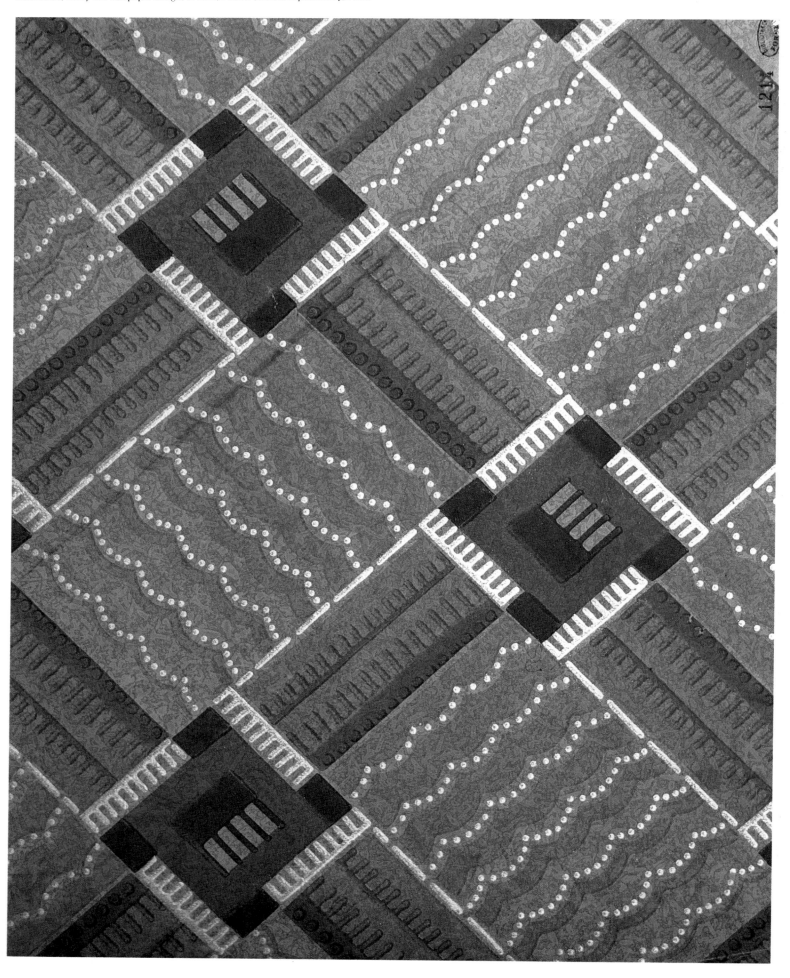

ANONYMOUS, *Leroy Co. wallpaper design, c. 1925, France (Bibliothèque Forney, Paris)*

ÉDOUARD BENEDICTUS, *"Les Fruits d'Or,"* textile design, 1925–30, France (Musée des Arts Décoratifs, Paris)

SONIA DELAUNAY, *"Tissu Simultané,"* textile design, 1926–27, France (Musée des Arts Décoratifs, Paris)

MISCELLANY

The proliferation of commercial activity after World War I created graphic design opportunities in many new areas. With the surge of popular music in the 1920s, sheet music became widely available. The covers gave music publishers an opportunity to illustrate and promote their products, and many Deco artists designed them, including the not-yet-surrealist René Magritte. American music covers were often cute and lighthearted in theme and execution, reflecting such titles as "A Cup of Coffee, a Sandwich, and You" and "Jim Jam Jems." The latter had an illustration by Fish that was used also as a cover for *Vanity Fair* in May 1920.* Netherlands artist L. O. Wenckeback produced one of the most impressive Cubist-inspired designs of the era for Leo Smit's "Suite pour le Piano"* in 1926.

Fans and matches were popular giveaways during the Deco years, promoting items ranging from shoes to department stores. Designs for some of these were created by important graphic artists such as Cappiello and Cassandre. One of the most beautiful fans, which used geometric patterning a year before the birth of Cubism, was produced by Josef Hoffmann* in Vienna in 1905.

When bridge became the rage in the twenties, many companies produced decorative playing cards with matching boxes and inventive bridge tallies.

JANY DESMET, *playing card, c. 1920–30, Belgium (Galerie DeWindt, Brussels)*

DELY, *"Ja, Bei den Hottentotten,"* sheet music cover, c. 1925, Germany (coll. Jamie Schler)

RENÉ VINCENT, *"Gitanes," bookmark, c. 1935, France (priv. coll.)*

E. MC KNIGHT-KAUFFER, *"T. E. Lawrence Ltd.," advertisements, 1921, Great Britain (priv. coll.)*

RENÉ MAGRITTE, *"Arlita" sheet music cover, c. 1925, Belgium (Galerie DeWindt, Brussels)*

ANONYMOUS, *bridge tallies, Craftacre Co., c. 1935, U.S.A. (Primavera Gallery, New York)*

A. M. CASSANDRE, *"Dubo . . . Dubon . . . Dubonnet," fan based on poster, 1932, France (Primavera Gallery, New York)*

ANONYMOUS, *"Shiseido Ice Cream Parlor," matchbox label, 1925–35, Japan (Shiseido Cosmetics, Tokyo)*

NOVO (NELLO VOLTOLINO), *"Nostalgia di Greta," sheet music cover, 1931, Italy*

ANONYMOUS, *"Gabriel Ferot," fan, c. 1925–30, France (Duvelleroy Galerie, Paris)*

PAUL IRIBE, *fan based on book illustration, c. 1920, France (Duvelleroy Galerie, Paris)*

ANONYMOUS, *"Body and Soul," sheet music cover, c. 1930, France (priv. coll.)*

LEON ULLMAN, *"La Note Juste,"* c. 1930, France (priv. coll.)

L. O. WENCKEBACH, *"Suite pour le Piano,"* *sheet music cover, 1926, France (John Vloemans Antiquarian Books, The Hague)*

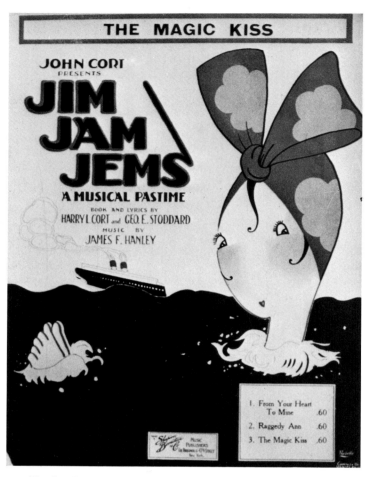

FISH, *"Jim Jam Jems," sheet music cover, c. 1925, U.S.A. (priv. coll.)*

LABOCCETTA, *"S.S. Paris," menu cover, 1930, France (Musée des Arts Décoratifs, Paris)*

JOSEF HOFFMANN, *"Fan with Phantasiearchitekturen," printed silk, c. 1905, Austria (Bellerive Museum, Zurich)*

227

RENE MAGRITTE, *"Le Tango des Aveux,"* sheet music cover, c. 1925, Belgium (coll. Brigitte Homburg)

228

ANONYMOUS, *playing cards, Park Avenue Playing Card Co., c. 1935, U.S.A. (Primavera Gallery, New York)*

The Art Deco era was an extraordinarily rich period for the production of outstanding books, perhaps the most exciting since the time of the medieval manuscripts. While many superbly designed and printed books were produced in the four and a half centuries following the introduction of printing in Europe, it was only when the advance of printing, papermaking, and color-reproduction technology reached the level it did in the twentieth century that it was possible to publish books in large numbers with a richness of color illustration and design comparable to that of the illuminated manuscripts. This combined with the simultaneous explosion of innovation and public interest in art to provide a fertile ground for the flowering of books that in every sense reflected modernism—the twentieth-century style that became Art Deco.

Modernism in European book design

Despite a propitious climate, the spirit of modernism had a difficult time penetrating book design. This was a field in which conservatism had prevailed for centuries, in large part because book design was mainly in the hands of printers rather than graphic designers. Few printers were designers by talent or training, and their work tended to be bounded by the physical limits of metal-type composition. Consequently, centered arrangements of traditional serifed roman typefaces dominated the art.

A few radical designers, mostly from outside the book field, brought the ideas of de Stijl, the Bauhaus, and Constructivism to books. Designers such as
29 Herbert Bayer, El Lissitzky, Piet Zwart,* and Kurt Schwitters introduced asymmetrical arrangements of sans-serif faces, often in strongly contrasting weights, and didn't hesitate to slant, curve, or "bounce" lines of type.

Two interesting designs related to particular avant-garde movements are the
251 1928 composition* by Czech designer Karel Teige, reminiscent of Constructivism, and the cover for *Opere Pubbliche* by the Italian A. Calzavara, which extends the lettering to create a Futurist image of speed.

These innovations might have had a salutary effect, shaking the book world out of its torpor, but in fact they succeeded mainly in horrifying the conservative. The modernists' failure to effect broad changes in book design probably was due to the extreme nature of their early efforts. This failure was represented in the career of Jan Tschichold, who switched to a traditional style in the early forties and for the rest of his life decried the radical typography of his youth.

The Art Deco typographic style was seen in books not so much in layout as in

A. CALZAVARA, Opere Pubbliche 1922–1932, *book cover, 1934, Italy (from the Mitchell Wolfson Jr. Collection of Decorative and Propaganda Arts, Miami)*

the use of typefaces that represented the era, including, to some extent, the sans-serif type designs and the modified sans-serifs.

Modernism in American book design

If modernism in books had a hard time getting accepted in Europe, where it began, it made almost no impact in America. The only American book designer who contributed significantly to the Art Deco style was W. A. Dwiggins. His "strange" decorations and drawings, as he called them, were entirely at home with the decorative elements of Art Deco architecture and interior design. Dwiggins was a superb calligrapher and letterer, and even though he never thought of his work as modernist, his letter forms had the Deco spirit. He was actually quite conservative in designing book pages, and his page layout rarely attempted the modernist style, but his cover for *The* 249 *Power of Print—and Men** (1936) is full of energy and diversity. A large chapter heading that occupies half the page echoes the geometric patterning. Dwiggins, like McKnight-Kauffer in England, was an illustrator-designer with a special affinity for book work.

230

S. A. Jacobs, Merle Armitage, Ernst Reichl, and one or two other American designers produced books in the modernist mode during the thirties, although little of this work had the Art Deco feeling that pervaded Dwiggins's work. The brilliant magazine art director Alexey Brodovitch designed a few outstanding books, but these were occasional works from outside the book publishing world.

MERLE ARMITAGE, Igor Strawinsky, *edited by Merle Armitage, title page, 1935, U.S.A.*

Modernism in jackets

The Deco style was more easily assimilated in book jackets, which were considered promotional devices rather than part of the book. Less subject to the technological limitations of letterpress printing, they escaped the iron hand of tradition that controlled book design. Many contemporary jackets had characteristics of Deco graphic style, but unfortunately the pay for jacket designs was very low, so they were rarely done by first-rank artists, and then they tended to be dashed off with relatively little effort. A few examples are jackets for *The Weekend Book* by McKnight-Kauffer, *Daughters of India* by Lee Elliot, and *Cullum* by A. Paxton Chadwick.

The illustrated book: France

Art Deco style found its way into books more through illustration than page design, and then more in the "éditions de luxe" than in commercially produced and distributed books. In the Art Deco era, the production of beautifully illustrated books was encouraged and often financed by organizations of French book enthusiasts, such as the Société des Bibliophiles Français, the Société des Amis des Livres, the Société des Bibliophiles Contemporains, the Cent Bibliophiles, and the Société du Livre Contemporain. The last would typically commission an artist and then choose a literary work to suit his style—often having the translation made by a leading literary figure. Exquisite tooled-leather bindings were commissioned also, although often books were sold unbound, leaving the buyer free to have a binding made to his own taste. The binding as well as the rest of the book frequently reflected the Deco graphic style at its best. Publication of the Société's books was usually celebrated by an elaborate dinner party.

ALEXANDER ALEXEIEFF, The Brothers Karamazov *by Fyodor Dostoevski, book cover, 1929, France*

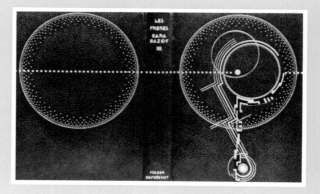

Most of the artists who illustrated these books were known for their fashion, theater, and magazine work, but a few did a major part of their work in books. They ranged from some of the leading avant-garde artists to professional illustrators.

French art dealer and publisher Ambroise Vollard commissioned many important artists to illustrate a number of extraordinary books. While neither the design nor the illustrations of these books—illustrated by such as Picasso, Léger, Roualt, and Matisse—were particularly Art Deco in style, they embodied the spirit of the time in both their extravagant quality and their modernist sensibility. Today they stand as shining examples of the creative union of art and literature. A noteworthy volume is Blaise Cendrars's *La Fin du Monde* illustrated by Léger in 1919, in which the ingenious design reflects Cubism as well as the Art Deco style. The page "Le Truc"* shows the infatuation with black jazz; another page, "L'Ange Opérateur,"* has an intricate Dadaist arrangement of letters; the cover is a challenging typographic design.

267
266

The illustrated book: England and America

A "fine book" movement developed in England and America, parallel to the "éditions de luxe" activity in France. In both countries there were a considerable number of private presses that turned out creditable books. More significant, however, were the Nonesuch Press in Britain, directed by Francis Meynell, and the American Limited Editions Club under George Macy. Both publishers commissioned the best artists of the time to illustrate classics and contemporary works, and sold the books by subscription, usually for a series. They differed from the French practice by emphasizing the use of machine production rather than handwork—a typical art–industry marriage of the era. As a result of this and their more commercial approach to distribution, their books were comparatively inexpensive.

Many of the French Deco artists illustrated these books. American and British illustrators with modernist styles were few, but there were some notable volumes in this mode, including *Benito Cereno* (1926), illustrated for Nonesuch by McKnight-Kauffer, and the Limited Edition Club's *Looking Backward* (1941), designed by Merle Armitage.

Pochoir: a brief but brilliant life

In the Art Deco period publishers frequently used the pochoir (stencil) process to reproduce illustrations. The process required extremely skilled craftsmanship and produced very beautiful results. In some cases artists themselves did work using pochoir as a medium.

In pochoir (as in silk-screen printing), stencils separated the colors for reproduction. The colors, both opaque and transparent, were applied by hand, by daubing, spraying, stippling, or sponging to achieve various effects. Sometimes black outlines were first printed by lithography. The concept of pochoir is simple, but the application can be very complicated and time-consuming. However, the result is stunning: vibrantly rich colors, often indistinguishable from original watercolors and gouaches.

Artists, publishers, and the public were captivated by the remarkable reproductions. The pochoir rage began in 1908, with Paul Poiret's small fashion album illustrated by Iribe. Following that there were albums printed with

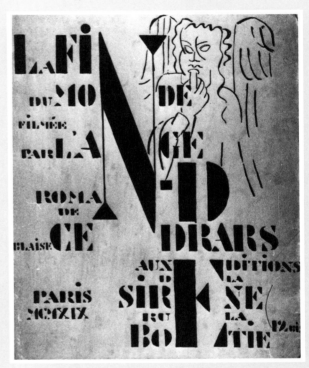

FERNAND LÉGER, La Fin du Monde *by Blaise Cendrars, book cover, 1919, France (John Vloemans Antiquarian Books, The Hague)*

pochoir reproduction of illustrations by Barbier, Lepape, Martin, and Marty. The success of these books stimulated interest in, and extensive use of, the process in all fields of graphics at the time.

To produce his portfolio *Le Tumulte Noir* (c. 1930), which chronicled Parisians' fascination with Josephine Baker and jazz, Paul Colin is said to have hand-colored by pochoir the entire edition of 500 copies. Sonia Delaunay was drawn to the fashion industry, and her *Ses Peintures, Ses Objets, Ses Tissus Simultanés, Ses Modes,** with an introduction by André Lhote, was published to coincide with the 1925 Paris Exposition. The twenty pictures, based on designs from as early as 1912, were magnificent illustrations for women's clothes, children's dresses, theatrical costumes, and fabrics, all reproduced by pochoir. Exquisite portfolios printed by pochoir include Léon Bakst's *Synthèse de l'Œuvre du Maître* (1928), with costumes for *The Sleeping Beauty* and other plays. Thirty-one designs by Picasso for the Ballets Russes production *Le Tricorne* were published in an edition of 250 in 1920.

232

PAUL COLIN, Le Tumulte Noir *by Paul Colin, book illustration, 1929, France (Leonard Fox Rare Books, New York)*

Some fabric and wallpaper pattern designs, primarily by E. A. Seguy and Édouard Benedictus, were printed by pochoir in the 1920s and were so beautiful that they were sold as art portfolios. Benedictus's portfolios *Projet de Boîtes Laquées** and *Relais* were among many in which he enlivened floral and abstract designs with imaginative, often electric, colors. Seguy was his equal. His work, still influenced by Art Nouveau, was not so geometric, but he produced flamboyant pochoir albums, such as *Papillon*, on butterflies, and *Samarkande*, which showed exotic plants. These works, applied to textiles, wallpaper, book bindings, tapestries, and packaging, stimulated the imagination of other designers and illustrators.

The use of pochoir was centered in France, but it was used also in England and other countries. In Russia it was used to reproduce Vladimir Lebedev's illustrations for *Fenêtre Rosta** (1925), which depicted the new bourgeoisie and the army defending the borders.

Several factors—the need for mass production, advances in color printing, the Depression, and World War II—combined to end the widespread use of pochoir as a reproduction process. Today pochoir is nearly a lost art.

Book artists of the Art Deco era

SCHMIED

François-Louis Schmied was a phenomenal book artist whose important works are, unaccountably, known mainly by comparatively few dealers, collectors, and scholars. His exquisite illustrations and page designs are pure Art Deco style. He was able to assimilate all of the tendencies and sources of the style—the elongation of figures, the geometricism, the eccentric arrangements, the transformations of reality—and evolve a personal style of virtually unmatched beauty. The Société du Livre Contemporain commissioned two of his outstanding works, Alfred de Vigny's *Daphné* (1925) and *La Création* (1928), an excerpt from the book of Genesis. It is noteworthy that Schmied's use in *Daphné** of a monumental single initial to dominate the page echoed a practice of the medieval manuscript artists—but with a distinctly Art Deco style and character.

Schmied was obsessive about controlling every detail of his books; he not only selected the paper, designed the pages, and made the illustrations, he also cut the illustrations in wood; designed his own typefaces, sometimes creating a face specifically for one book; printed the books on his own press; and often designed the bindings. Even with help, it typically took Schmied two to three years to produce a book in an edition of 25 to 175 copies. He was a secretive craftsman who would not permit anyone to watch him work.

Schmied's early life is obscure, but he probably worked as a printer's apprentice in Geneva before moving to Paris around the turn of the century, following his close friend, the lacquerist Jean Dunand. He was at first a technician, and was considered the best wood engraver in the city. He cut in wood illustrations by the best artists. During World War I Schmied lost an eye, but his skill did not seem to suffer. It was not until 1923, when he was fifty, that he began to do book illustration. His first book was *Salammbô* by Flaubert. Its impressive Cubist designs won him further commissions.

According to rare-book authority Leonard Fox, when the illustrations from Schmied's *Daphné* were exhibited at the Maison des Artistes de Paris around 1925, "a revelation occurred." These works created a sensation, like Duchamp's *Nude Descending a Staircase*. Schmied became immensely popular among collectors, and some of his books sold for the equivalent of three thousand dollars today, a fortune at that time.

It is said that Schmied and Dunand had expensive tastes; they jointly owned a yacht, and enjoyed gambling. The heavy spending came to a halt with the Depression, when sumptuous books became unaffordable and Schmied went bankrupt. In his last years Schmied was given a government job, but he died virtually in poverty in 1941.

Ironically, it was probably Schmied's great success in his lifetime that caused his present relative obscurity. The very high cost of his books so limited their distribution that they were seen by too few to establish a wide reputation, particularly as they were printed in very small editions.

LABOUREUR, LABORDE, VERTÈS

Jean-Émile Laboureur was the most Art Deco of the many important French book illustrators. He moved to Paris in 1895 and received advice from Toulouse-Lautrec; his distinct style shows a freedom in drawing with quick
260 simple lines, like Lautrec. Laboureur* created a sense of agitation, characteristic of the Deco era, with shadows, figures, and objects pitched at varying angles. His elongated people always seemed carefree and sociable, even during the war years. Two examples of his books are *L'Envers du Music-Hall* by Colette (1926) and *La Saison au Bois de Boulogne* by Maurice Beaubourg (1928).

120 The mood was quite different in the work of Charles Laborde,*who was anguished by the depersonalization of modern life, and strove to give his characters distinct personalities. Marcel Vertès, a Hungarian who lived in Vienna before settling in Paris, produced many book illustrations with an Art Deco flavor, including a much sought after portfolio (*Dancings* [1925]) of Parisian night life, *Les Six Étages* by Gérard Bauer, *L'Amour Vénal* (1926) by Colette, and *L'Âge d'Or* (1926) by Georges-Armand Masson.

Bottom
F.-L. SCHMIED, Daphné *by Alfred de Vigny, page design and illustration, 1924, France (Leonard Fox Rare Books, New York)*

Below
F.-L. SCHMIED, *"La Serpentine," book illustration for* La Création, *1928, France (Félix Marcilhac, Paris)*

The four major French fashion artists—Barbier, Lepape, Martin, and Marty—all illustrated literary books as well as fashion albums during the Art Deco period. Whereas specialization prevails today, it was understood at that time that an artist was capable of performing well in several fields. It was not uncommon for an architect to do graphic design or for an illustrator to design textiles or for any artist to illustrate books, even though his reputation was established in another field.

Barbier had a passion for Greek vases, and, especially in his work prior to 1920, the classical influence was evident in his drawings, despite his clear inclination toward Art Deco simplification. Even later on he subtly introduced winged cherubs and other romantic touches into his distinctly modernist drawings. In his 1923 illustration "Incantation,"* for the annual *Falbalas et Fanfreluches*, Barbier was at his best, creating beautiful women who were at once innocent and sophisticated. His characters were always impeccably dressed and perfectly posed, seemingly without a care. His women were slim and sweet at the beginning, but became less delicate and more chic over the years. His men tended to be languid and dapper, usually wearing evening clothes.

261

Barbier loved the dance and illustrated many books on the subject, including *Dances de Nijinsky* (1913). He illustrated *Les Chansons de Bilitis* by Pierre Louÿs (1922), *Le Carrosse aux Deux Lézards Verts* by René Boylesve (1921), *Falbalas et Fanfreluches* (almanacs, 1922–26), *Le Bonheur du Jour ou les Grâces à la Mode* (1924), *Fêtes Galantes* by Verlaine (1928), and *Poèmes en Prose* by Maurice de Guérin (1928). Barbier had produced twenty-five illustrations for Louÿs's *Aphrodite* when he died in 1932. Lepape completed the work (Schmied engraved the illustrations).

Lepape was the most stylized and elegant of the four, often setting extremely elongated bodies in sharply angled poses, with hands on the hips or heads tilted at an uncomfortable angle. His women's eyes were evasive, and either had an Oriental look or were made of wide circles, always with much colorful eye makeup rimmed in black. He liked long, boxy necks and long fingers, and used vivid oranges, greens, and blues. Lepape slipped into the Deco style quickly, employing simplification and geometricism from the beginning, as *Les Choses de Paul Poiret Vues par Georges Lepape* (1911) demonstrates. The background is a garden of circular and triangular hedges. The woman is sophisticated and stylized. A characteristic special touch is the dots in the eyes and around the eye shadow to repeat the dots in the turban. Lepape illustrated the complete works of Alfred de Musset and *L'Oiseau Bleu* by Maeterlinck (1925), and contributed to the annual *Modes et Manières d'Aujourd'hui* (1912–23).

Martin became the most distinctly cubistic of the four after the war, often using light lines to create overlapping geometrical forms. His characters tended to have a cartoonish quality, each with a distinct, humorous personality. He liked erotic touches in his commercial work, such as a woman at a party with one breast exposed, and was known for his erotic drawings. His books included *Nounette* by Henri Duvernois (1912), *Sports et Divertissements* by Erik Satie (1923), *Contes Vénitiens* by Henri de Régnier (1927), *Pierrot Fumiste* by Jules Laforgue (1927), and *Mascarades et Amusettes*

GEORGES LEPAPE, Les Choses de Paul Poiret Vues par Georges Lepape, *book illustration, 1911, France (priv. coll.)*

265 (1930). "La Passerelle,"* for the 1913 edition of *Modes et Manières d'Aujourd'hui*, is one of his more subdued works, but the sharp angles created by the pitch of the tree trunk, the tree leaves, and the boat and cars make it lively. As in most of Martin's works, the woman is experienced, poised, and determined, with knowing almond eyes and a sharp nose.

Marty, like the others, was a prolific book illustrator. His style rested somewhere between Barbier's and Lepape's, incorporating more geometricism and simplification than Barbier but retaining the girlish naïveté of the Barbier woman. His books included *Daphnis et Alaimadure* by La Fontaine (1926), *Le Diadème de Flore* by Gérard d'Houville (1928), *Les Poésies de Méléagre* by Louÿs (1933), and *Ernestine, ou la Naissance de l'Amour* by Stendhal (1939).

SAUVAGE, AGHION

Some books of the period were favorites, with several editions illustrated by different artists. For instance, *Les Chansons de Bilitis* was illustrated by Barbier in 1922, Sylvain Sauvage in 1927, and Janine Aghion about 1920 (not published). While Sauvage's style is quite different from that of "the four," it is distinctly Art Deco. Among his books are *Les Liaisons Dangereuses* by S. Laclos (1930), *Le Florilège des Dames* (written by Sauvage; 1932), and *Naissance de l'Odyssée* by S. Giono (1935). One of his illustrations from *Les*
268 *Chansons de Bilitis** shows a simplified, tubular woman in repose, with a touch of geometry at the bottom right.

Aghion's "La Partie d'Osselets" for *Les Chansons de Bilitis* shows her free, loose style, which leaned toward abstraction. Her finished work looked as though she drew quickly and spontaneously, with less emphasis on careful composition than most artists of the period, but she was a particularly inventive colorist. Little is known of Aghion, whose works are few, but it is established that she designed alongside Erté in Poiret's couture house. Her charm-
280 ing *Essence of the Mode of the Day** (1920) shows her advanced, elongated style in stretched figures reminiscent of those of Van Dongen, such as the
254 elastic diving bather.* This edition contained sixteen illustrations of women participating in sports, a reflection of the emphasis on the new freedom of
257 women. In *Grain de Poivre** (1927) by Franz Toussaint, Aghion placed a beautiful sleeping woman on a sea of circular cushions and structures, a typical Art Deco bow to geometry.

JANINE AGHION, *"La Partie d'Osseletes," book illustration for an unpublished edition of* Les Chansons de Bilitis *by Pierre Louÿs, c. 1920, France (Jadis et Naguère, Paris)*

ERIC GILL, ALASTAIR

264 One of the most notable English illustrators was Eric Gill.* He was a sculptor, engraver, writer, and typographer. A radical by inclination, Gill, like most British artists, could not fully give up the longstanding traditions of the book; his work never quite had a modernist feeling, although many of his illustrations were influenced by the vanguard art movements. It is curious that although Gill was deeply religious, his illustrations were often erotic and considered indecent by much of the public. The true successor to England's blatantly erotic, "decadent" Aubrey Beardsley was the illustrator Alastair.
260 In his 1925 book illustration,* the elongated, tubular body draped with jewels is also reminiscent of Erté.

ROCKWELL KENT

In the United States, Rockwell Kent had the most dramatic Art Deco style. He illustrated many books, including *Candide* (1928), *Moby Dick* (1930), and *Beowulf and the Dragon* (1932). Like Gill, he had a strong affinity for the past. His favorite artist was William Blake, and he signed some of his humorous pictures "Hogarth, Jr." Kent was a versatile artist who also did numerous illustrations for advertisements as well as magazines and books.

Art Deco book art in Europe

During the Art Deco era there were many excellent book artists working in every European country, in addition to those already mentioned, and some of them produced work in the modernist mode. Among these are Italy's Giulio
246   Cisari, Portugal's Souza-Cardosa, Russia's V. Lebedev* and P. Pavlinov,
264   Denmark's Kay Nielsen,* Germany's Erich Heckel and Karl Schmidt, France's Édouard Chimot and Gustav Végh, and Czechoslovakia's
243/258   Hlaváček.* A particularly interesting book is the 3 × 3″ *Die Nibelungen*,* published in Vienna in 1920, with illustrations by Carl Otto Czeschka. Also unusual is the photomontage cover by architect Le Corbusier for his book
250   *Des Canons, des Munitions** (1937). If a preponderance of the artists and books discussed in this chapter are French, it is mainly because the Art Deco style developed in France—actually, in Paris—and that is where many artists from the rest of Europe went to live and work for a variety of reasons, many having to do with adverse economic or political conditions in their homelands. Those conditions also limited the spread of Art Deco and handicapped the production of books.

ROCKWELL KENT, Leaves of Grass *by Walt Whitman, book illustration, 1936, U.S.A.*

GUSTAV VÉGH, Calligrammes *by Guillaume Appollinaire, book cover, France*

C. O. CZESCHKA, Die Nibelungen *by F. Keim, book illustration, 1920, Austria (priv. coll.)*

JEAN CARLU, *Philippe de Rothschild bookplate, c. 1929, France (priv. coll.)*

CHARLES MARTIN, *endpapers, c. 1915, France (Bibliothèque Forney, Paris)*

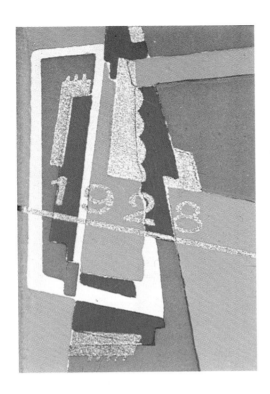

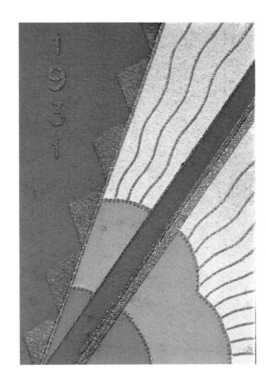

ANONYMOUS, *almanac covers, approx. 2½ × 3¾", France (coll. Sacha Leroy, Bibliothèque Forney, Paris)*

FISH, High Society *by Fish, book cover, 1915, U.S.A. (priv. coll.)*

FISH, **High Society** *by Fish, endpapers, 1915, U.S.A. (priv. coll.)*

BART VAN DER LECK, *Madeleine bookplate, c. 1925, The Netherlands*
(John Vloemans Antiquarian Books, The Hague)

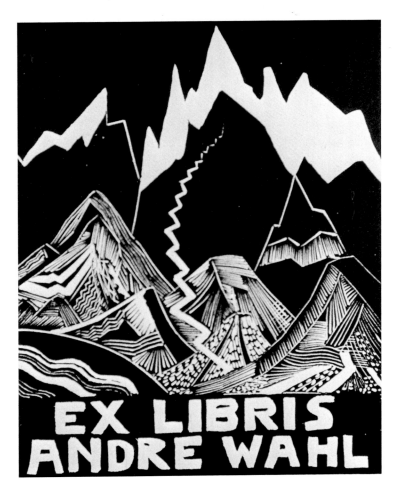

ANONYMOUS, *André Wahl, bookplate (priv. coll.)*

EL LISSITZKY, Das Entfesselte Theatre *by Alexander Tairoff, book
cover, 1927, Germany (John Vloemans Antiquarian Books, The
Hague)*

HLAVAČK, Růžové Viry *by J. Landa, book cover, 1927, Czechoslovakia (John Vloemans Antiquarian Books, The Hague)*

F.-L. SCHMIED, Daphné *by Alfred de Vigny, book illustration, 1924, France (Leonard Fox Rare Books,*
New York)

oraison que quelques phrases bri-
sées par ses bégaiements. Julien
s'avança. Il avait été ordonné lec-
teur de l'Église en même temps
que son frère ; mais, plus ardent
dans sa piété, il s'était fait tonsu-
rer, et il était moine. Revêtu de la

F.-L. SCHMIED, Daphné *by Alfred de Vigny, book page design and illustration, 1924, France (Leonard*
Fox Rare Books, New York)

VLADIMIR LEBEDEV, La Chasse et la Pêche, *album cover*

MAN RAY, Le Surréalisme et la Peinture *by André Breton, book cover, 1928, France (priv. coll.)*

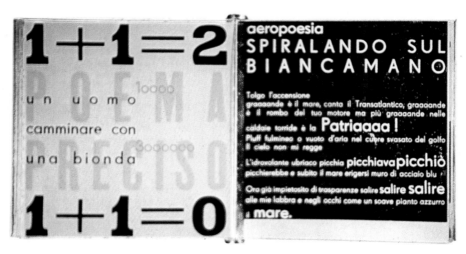

TULLIO D'ALBISOLA, **Parole in Libertà** *by F. T. Marinetti, book page designs, 1932, Italy*

W. A. DWIGGINS, **The Power of Print and Men** *by Thomas Dreier, book cover, 1936, U.S.A.*

LE CORBUSIER, Des Canons, des Munitions *by Le Corbusier, book cover, 1937, France (John Vloemans
Antiquarian Books, The Hague)*

ANONYMOUS, Agenda PLM, *book cover, 1929, France (Bibliothèque Forney, Paris)*

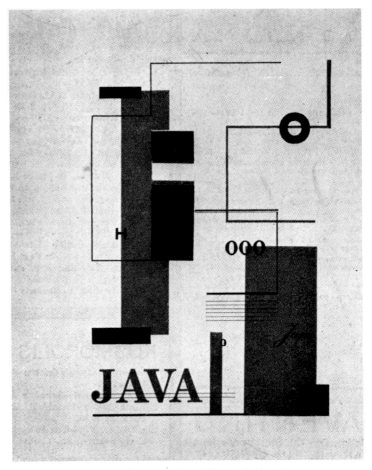

KAREL TEIGE, Java, *typographic composition, 1928, Czechoslovakia (priv. coll.)*

MOUSYKA, *bookplates, c. 1930, Russia (Musée des Arts Décoratifs, Paris)*

SONIA DELAUNAY, *portfolio illustration, "Ses Peintures, Ses Objets, Ses Tissus Simultanés, Ses Modes," c. 1925, France (Leonard Fox Rare Books, New York)*

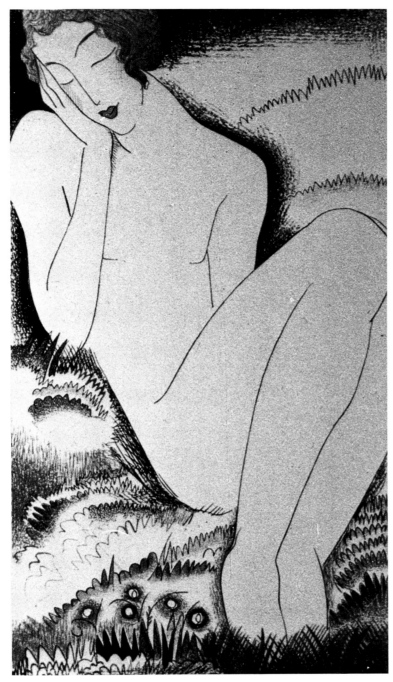

F.-L. SCHMIED, La Création, *tr. by J. C. Mardrus, book illustration,*
1928, France (Leonard Fox Rare Books, New York)

253

ÉDOUARD BENEDICTUS, Projet de Boîtes Laquees, *c. 1925, France*
(Jadis et Naguère, Paris)

F.-L. SCHMIED, Le Paradis Musulman, *tr. by J. C. Mardrus, book illustration, 1930 (Leonard Fox Rare Books, New York)*

JANINE AGHION, **The Essence of the Mode of the Day**, *book illustration, 1920, France (coll. Susan J. Pack)*

F.-L. SCHMIED, La Création, *tr. by J. C. Mardrus, book illustration, 1928, France (Leonard Fox Rare Books, New York)*

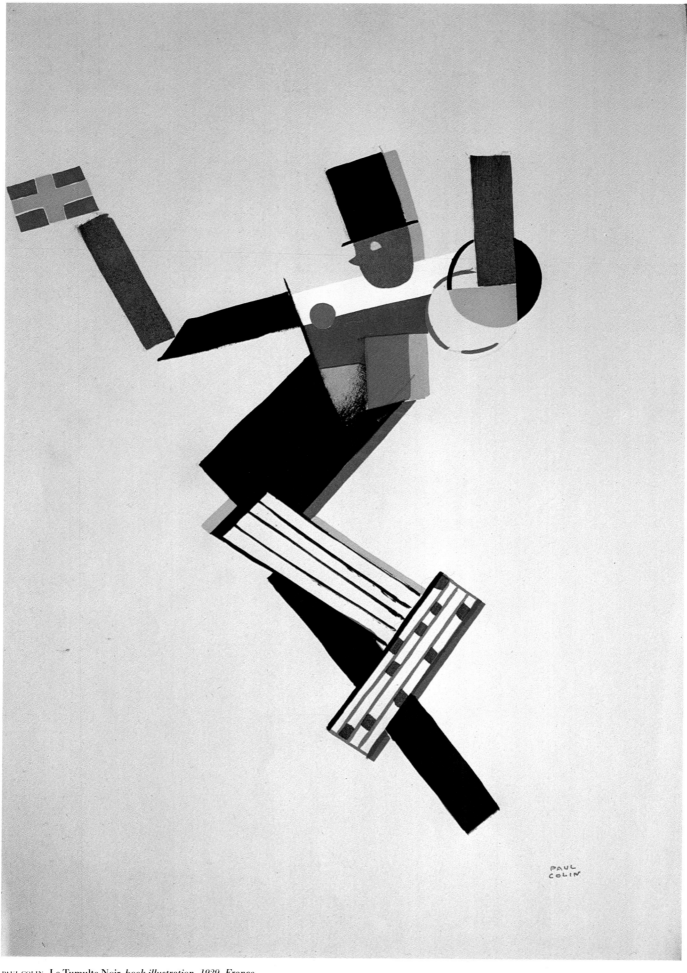

PAUL COLIN, Le Tumulte Noir, *book illustration, 1929, France*
(Leonard Fox Rare Books, New York)

JANINE AGHION, **Grain de Poivre** *by Franz Toussaint, book illustration, France (Leonard Fox Rare Books, New York)*

C. O. CZESCHKA, Die Nibelungen *by F. Keim, book illustration, 1920, Austria (priv. coll.)*

C. O. CZESCHKA, Die Nibelungen *by F. Keim, book illustration, 1920, Austria (priv. coll.)*

ROCKWELL KENT, Glory, Glory, *lithograph, 1944, illustration for book jacket,* American Voices *by Walter Lorrenfels (1959), U.S.A. (Associated American Artists, New York)*

J.-É. LABOUREUR, *"The Trenches in the Village,"* book illustration, 1916, France (Jadis et Naguère, Paris)

ALASTAIR, *"A Slave,"* book illustration, 1925, U.S.A. (Galerie Bernd Dürr, Munich)

GEORGE BARBIER, *"Incantation," book illustration for* Falbalas et Fanfreluches, *1923, France (Jadis et Naguère, Paris)*

SONIA DELAUNAY, *portfolio illustration*, *"Ses Peintures, Ses Objets, Ses Tissus Simultanés, Ses Modes,"* c. 1925, France (Leonard Fox Rare Books, New York)

LYND WARD, *"Wall Street,"* woodcut illustration from Vertigo by Lynd Ward, 1937, U.S.A. (Associated American Artists, New York)

VLADIMIR LEBEDEV, *"The New Bourgeoisie in Russia," book illustration for* Fenêtre Rosta, *1925, Russia (John Vloemans Antiquarian Books, The Hague)*

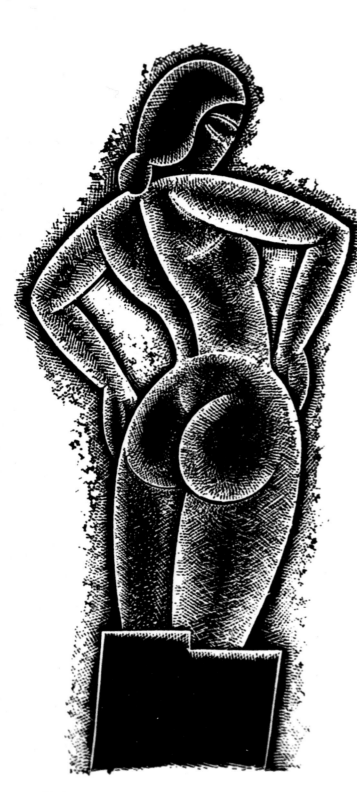

ERIC GILL, *"Sculpture No. 2," wood engraving, 1930*

GUSTAVE BUCHET, Les Amies, Filles *by Verlaine, book illustration, 1921, France*

KAY NIELSEN, Sous le Signe du Rossignol *by Henri Jacques, book illustration, 1923, France*

CHARLES MARTIN, *"La Passarelle," illustration for* Modes et Manières d'Aujourd'hui, *1913, France*
(Jadis et Naguère, Paris)

FERNAND LÉGER, *"L'Ange Operateur," book illustration for* La Fin du Monde *by Blaise Cendrars, 1919,*
France (John Vloemans Antiquarian Books, The Hague)

FERNAND LÉGER, *"Le Truc," book illustration for* La Fin du Monde *by Blaise Cendrars, 1919, France*
(John Vloemans Antiquarian Books, The Hague)

SYLVAIN SAUVAGE, **Les Chansons de Bilitis** *by Pierrre Louÿs, book illustration, c. 1925, France (Jadis et Naguère, Paris)*

Fashion and Costume

During that unique period in history, the Art Deco era, a free-spirited inter-change among all the arts occurred. Some of the most prominent avant-garde talents created fashions, costumes, and sets, as well as designs in graphics, jewelry, and other areas. Fashion and costume were enriched and revolution-ized by this intense and adventurous activity. Important painters such as Léger, De Chirico, and Picasso were involved with the theater; Sonia Delaunay, Stepanova, Dufy, Hoffmann, and Malevich with fabric design; Magritte, Dali, Van Dongen, Foujita, and Laurencin did work associated with fashion. Architects who had been in the vanguard since the turn of the century, as well as the Wiener Werkstätte and Deutsche Werkbund, had expanded the accepted concept of the artist's role, encouraging artistic creativity in all aspects of life. This attitude achieved realization at the Bauhaus, where students and teachers worked on theatrical presentations, painting, industrial designs, and typography simultaneously. Many designers of the period who created fashions and fashion illustrations produced the sets and costumes for operas, ballets, the legitimate theater, and cabaret revues, as well as Hollywood musical extravaganzas. While the theatrical sets and costumes have gone into storage or deteriorated with time, fashion graphics remain to document this important contribution to our culture.

FERNAND LÉGER, *costume design for* La Création du Monde, *Ballets Suédois, 1923, France*

The term "wearable art" could have been born during this period, for fashions were often exquisite works of art. By the second decade of the century fashion had developed to such a state of excellence that clothing was given its own exhibition space at the 1925 Paris Exposition. The foreword to the catalogue remarked, "this superiority [of French fashion design] rightly entitles fashion to a privileged showing."

Fashion follows freedom for women

It was no coincidence that this phenomenal period in fashion coincided with the growing freedom and independence of Western women. In fact, it would not have been possible without the advance in women's rights, and each development fueled the other. Although the seeds were planted long before, the right to vote, granted to women between 1918 and 1921 in France, England, and the United States, marked the official beginning of an era that would culminate in the women's movement of the 1960s. The dramatic changes in fashion occurring just before 1910 and extending throughout the Deco era became a major symbol of women's expanded opportunities for individuality, variety, and freedom of movement. By the 1920s the modern fashionable woman had taken center stage. The best fashion designers of the time let loose their imaginations and created for her some of the richest, most elegant, and most daring clothes ever seen.

Bakst and the Ballets Russes

The first performance of the Ballets Russes in Paris, on May 19, 1909, ignited the extraordinary developments in fashion and had far-reaching effects on the Art Deco movement. Season after season, this company electrified audiences, and was a major influence on Parisian life until the death, in 1939, of its great impresario, Serge Diaghilev. Energized by the opulent Russian productions, the public was eager to embrace the exotic settings of the ballets—whether Egyptian, Cubist, or Persian in theme. Couturiers were quick to incorporate into their fashions the ideas and images from these productions.

Diaghilev was gifted with the ability to bring creative geniuses together. In a communal atmosphere he put to work some of the most talented artists, composers, painters, writers, choreographers, sculptors, poets, and fashion illustrators (and, of course, dancers), many of whom were involved with ballet for the first time. One of the most striking assemblies of talent was gathered for the production of *Parade* in 1916, with Picasso as set and 277 costume designer;* Léonide Massine, choreographer; Jean Cocteau, writer; and Igor Stravinsky, composer. Diaghilev succeeded, in part, because he encouraged each contributor to express his ideas concerning the entire production, rather than concentrate only on his own area.

The Ballets Russes achieved extraordinary heights by combining exotic dancing and choreography by Nijinksy and others with the opulent, provoca- 289 tive costume and set designs of Léon Bakst.* "I never saw anything more beautiful," remarked Marcel Proust simply, commenting on Bakst's presentations. V. Svietlov, in his 1927 book *The Art of Bakst*, wrote: "Hundreds of costumes which filled the stage were all rivaling each other in originality and picturesqueness. He prepared a different curtain for every act. Each of them, with its original design, with its dazzling combinations of colors, was unanimously applauded by the public who admired the power of this creative genius, his inventiveness and taste. His talent was indefatigable; the treasury of his inventions was inexhaustible. He never repeated himself."

Bakst, whose first major introduction to Parisian audiences was with the Ballets Russes, designed costumes for both *Cléopatra* (1909) and *Schéhérazade* (1910), the two productions that had the most dramatic effects on fashion and on Art Deco in general.

The decadent, sumptuous aura of *Cléopatra* inspired Parisian women to shed their restricting corsets and let their clothing delineate their bodies. Dresses became light and sensuous, often flowing and clinging with a woman's movements, in imitation of Bakst's costumes for the ballet.

Schéhérazade was even more powerful than *Cléopatra*, memorable for its array of luxuriant colors. Emerald curtains, carpets from Bukhara, and plump silk cushions in exotic patterns adorned the stage. Billowing costumes in Persian blues, greens, oranges, and gold, with accents of rust and red, were draped in jewels, sashes, ribbons, and beads, producing a shimmering, dazzling spectacle.

Schéhérazade had a strong effect not only on fashion but on the entire field of interior decoration, especially textiles and wallpapers. Nightclubs and restaurants using the "Thousand and One Nights" theme appeared everywhere. Perfumes with Oriental names were announced, and colorful silk pillows for

LÉON BAKST, *"Narcisse," poster, 1911, France (Posters Please, New York)*

seating became popular, as did Paul Poiret's harem skirts, called "jupes-culottes," and the slender tunic. The ballet also influenced graphics. With sensitivity, Barbier captured the erotic sensuality of both Bakst's costumes and the dancer Nijinksy in a striking illustration of 1914. In the same year,

Barbier illustrated a gown called "Schéhérazade."* With its long waist, flowing fabric, and tall headdress with dangling pearls, the outfit was one of many that imitated Bakst's costumes. Erté's first cover for *Harper's Bazaar*, in 1915, was called "Schéhérazade," and the Casino de Paris produced the glittering revue *The Persian Carpet* in 1920.

Bakst's drawings for his costumes show his impressive flair for the exotic. The costumes themselves were spectacular, and they were illustrated by Bakst with a fluidity and richness unmatched by any other illustrator of the period. In addition to his work for the ballet, Bakst produced several illustrations for *Harper's Bazaar, La Gazette du Bon Ton*, and other magazines, and created designs for couturiers Worth and Paquin before he died in 1924.

GEORGE BARBIER, *"Nijinsky," illustration from* La Gazette du Bon Ton, *1914, France (Bibliothèque Forney, Paris)*

Poiret and the birth of modern fashion illustration

Inspired by Bakst's ingenious costumes, Poiret began to create daring, richly textured fashions in colorful fabrics. This couturier with an enormous flair for promotion was known for creating memorable evenings for his clients, such as his "Thousand and Second Night Ball" in 1911, for which he made costumes for several hundred guests. The opulent affair featured gold thrones, "slaves," "harem girls," wandering peacocks, Persian rugs, exotic music, and free-flowing Champagne.

As early as 1903 Poiret had understood women's readiness for freedom of movement and glamor, and he had been trying to promote a revolution in fashion. It was not until six years later that the revolution actually occurred, with the debut of the Ballets Russes. Clients had already begun abandoning their tight whalebone corsets in favor of his loose style, as well as adopting a brassiere he appropriately named "Liberty." In 1908 Poiret commissioned Paul Iribe, who had been drawing primarily caricatures, to illustrate a small book of his fashions to be given, or sold inexpensively, to his elite clientele. Choosing Iribe was a stroke of genius, for not only did the book have far-reaching effects on both men's careers, it inspired a new kind of graphic presentation of fashions and created a new type of fashion illustrator. Previously fashions had been drawn by technical illustrators who turned out realistic, straightforward presentations, faithfully reproducing every detail of a dress. Iribe drew in a linear style with simplification and elongation, techniques he had been using to illustrate fashion advertisements in his own publication, *Le Témoin (The Witness)*, the French answer to Germany's famous *Simplicissimus*. Poiret's fashions, as well as the illustrations he published, made other styles seem out of date. When the Ballets Russes came, what had been a slow evolution led by Poiret became an overnight revolution. Poiret became the reigning prince of fashion in Paris, and he inspired the creation of several magazines, including *La Gazette du Bon Ton*. He was not dethroned until the 1920s, when Coco Chanel became the leader of fashion trends with a totally new look that anticipated what is now recognized as the second phase of the development of Art Deco style: streamlining and a shift toward mass production.

The new use of color illustration was typified by Poiret's little hand-painted pochoir books. The use of the slow and expensive pochoir process for French magazines lasted until about 1925, when the leading publication, *La Gazette du Bon Ton*, ceased publication. The *Gazette* illustration "Après la Danse,"* built around a Worth dress, shows the effects of pochoir. A silver glitter added to the pink, black, and blue produces a luscious effect not possible in most conventional printing processes. In another example of elaborate illustration, "La Volière" by Martin, it is evident that both couturier and illustrator let their imaginations run free, creating a quite unwearable dress featuring birds in a cage. As time passed, fashion illustrators pushed the art to extremes. In Vladimir Bobritsky's October 1926 cover for *Vanity Fair*,* for instance, the woman's dress becomes almost incidental to the Constructivist stylization of trees and a greyhound.

285

304

Iribe is often overlooked in Art Deco fashion, but he laid a large part of its groundwork. A central, if less visible figure, he designed jewelry for Chanel and interiors for such notables as the entertainer Spinelly and the well-known couturier Jacques Doucet. He said in the publication *Choix*, "It seems that French fashion, as well as all the luxury industries that compose it, rediscovers that its goal is to help the woman in her eternal fight against time and to render her for a long time more moving and more beautiful." An example of the versatility of designers in the Deco era, Iribe designed objects, furniture, graphics, sets, and costumes, and became artistic director of many Broadway and Hollywood productions, most notably the Cecil B. De Mille extravaganza *The Ten Commandments*. His graphic work was sporadic, and he illustrated only when the need arose, as when he drew a languishing nude for the cover of Cocteau's short-lived magazine *Schéhérazade* (inspired by Rimsky-Korsakov's music a year before the premiere of the ballet). Ironically, Iribe was an important part of Poiret's career, and yet it was with Chanel, Poiret's successor as ruler of Paris fashion, that he fell in love.

Chanel: fashion enters the new age

Coco Chanel was the incomparable, enigmatic leader of international fashion in the 1920s, rivaled only by Elsa Schiaparelli in the 1930s. In 1922 Cocteau asked her to create the costumes for *Antigone* (with sets by Picasso) "because she is the greatest designer of our day." No one understood more clearly, or earlier, than Chanel that a major shift in design concepts was about to occur, with strong movements toward clean lines and mass production. She anticipated the emancipation of women and avoided designing only for the elite, as Poiret did. Like Diaghilev, whose later ballets (which she financially supported) embraced the avant-garde, Chanel drew inspiration from the modern art movements. Her designs reflected the streamlining and functionalism found in modernist architecture, Constructivism, and the Bauhaus, and she often gave her clothes a boxy shape, rather like simplified Cubism. Slim, classic, graceful, elegant, and often sporty, Chanel's signature fashions were styles that could be produced easily in large numbers by post–World War I manufacturers. By 1925 Poiret's elitist ideas of fashion were outmoded and he was bankrupt.

Fashion illustration and the modernist attitudes

The graphic artists continued to produce stunning illustrations. The December 15, 1925, cover of *Vogue* by Benito shows the fashion look at the height of

CHARLES MARTIN, *"La Volière," illustration from* La Gazette du Bon Ton, *c. 1915, France (Bibliothèque Forney, Paris)*

PAUL IRIBE, Schéhérazade *magazine cover, 1909, France (coll. Charles Spencer)*

E. G. BENITO, Vogue *magazine cover, December 1925, U.S.A. (priv. coll.)*

272

Art Deco. The attitude is one of modernist understatement, even though the dress is elaborately cut. The same attitude is shown in the artist's elongation of the model, making her appear streamlined. The Cubist geometricism of the patterned floor reinforces the modernist look. Fashion illustrators, like the posterists of the period, often created Cubist-inspired designs as the backdrop for fashions. A particularly creative example in grays and pinks is found in Reyaldo Luza's 1927–28 illustration* for furs. The erotically playful attitude of the 1920s toward fashion for the newly liberated woman is exposed in A. Vallée's cartoon for *La Vie Parisienne* in which a nearly topless woman hopes that her new dress will get her and her escort good seats.

297

Many of the important early fashion illustrators continued to work through the Art Deco period, adapting in various ways to the developing graphic style. One of these was Georges Lepape, a dominant figure in fashion as the most important cover illustrator for *Vogue*. He created hundreds of designs for that magazine over thirty years. His designs evolved toward a more simplified style, but he always retained the elongated body. His last cover for the publication, in 1938,* shows his perpetually lively imagination, with a dress created out of plaster to give it a three-dimensional effect. Lepape had been part of the corps of early *Gazette* illustrators and was especially important to Poiret, designing most of his books, posters, invitations, and advertisements, and even his letterhead. His counterpart was Erté, who had also started with Poiret as a designer, but went on to produce costumes, sets, and graphic designs, including hundreds of covers for *Vogue*'s competitor, *Harper's Bazaar*.*

301

127

A. VALLÉE, *"Le Déshabillé de Théâtre,"* illustration from La Vie Parisienne, c. 1925, France (priv. coll.)

Fashion illustration and the theater

Lepape, Erté, and other important fashion illustrators spread their talents into many different areas, particularly the entertainment world. Lepape, for instance, designed for the Ballets Russes. He also created a poster for Spinelly* in 1914, which showed the actress's face in close-up, setting off a new trend. Erté, however, had the most important career in the theater during the 1920s and 1930s, when the French musical revues were at their peak. He designed costumes for the famous Mistinguett and in the mid-1920s won plaudits with his glittering outfits for the Folies-Bergère production of *Les Bijoux des Perles*, among others. Like many fashion-theatrical designers, Erté went to New York to work for the *Ziegfeld Follies* and *George White's Scandals*, and then on to Hollywood. He then designed a collection of fabrics for the Amalgamated Silk Corporation in New York.

282

ERTÉ, *illustration from* Harper's Bazaar, *February 1916, U.S.A. (priv. coll.)*

Of the many fashion illustrators of the period, it was Erté who best adapted Bakst's exotic designs to the illustration of fashion revues. His subjects were draped in flowing jewels, surrounded with fur, and engulfed in soft, billowing fabric. However, although his designs are dramatic, and certainly more exquisite than most other artists' designs, they are more like set pieces in comparison with Bakst's animated style.

The visual effects for these French revues were no small undertaking. Often a show needed a thousand or more spectacular costumes, complete with jewelry, headdresses, trains, shoes, and the stage sets to show them off. One of the most gifted designers was Charles Gesmar, who was so consumed by the demands of the stage that his graphic work was only incidental to his artistic output for revues. However, his many posters of Mistinguett,* for

101

whom he designed almost exclusively for more than ten years, remain graphic classics. One of his most spectacular creations was his 1924 poster showing his "Bird of Paradise" costume for Mistinguett, with plumes and a long feather train. Another poster, "The Jewels," captured the exciting entertainer when she was past fifty years old.

The connection with the theater was strong among other fashion illustrators, including Barbier, Martin, Marty, Zig, and Umberto Brunelleschi. The last worked for many French and American magazines, including *Fémina*, *Journal des Dames et des Modes*, and *Harper's Bazaar*, as well as several Italian publications. Brunelleschi was a regular costume designer for Josephine Baker, who was still adored by audiences in the 1930s. Although his graphic work is scant and somewhat uneven, at its best it is among the most exciting by the illustrators of the period.

Barbier was very interested in the theater, and illustrated numerous books with entertainment themes. At times, like other artists of his period, he designed every aspect of a performance, as well as graphics to promote it. For example, for Maurice Rostand's 1919 play *Casanova*, Barbier designed all the costumes and produced a book illustrating twenty-four of its scenes and costumes. However, while he designed costumes for the Folies-Bergère and the Casino de Paris, as well as many theatrical plays, he devoted himself primarily to his illustrations.

Fashion illustration in advertising

In the 1920s and 1930s fashion became big business, and advertising pages were filled with promotions for beauty products, perfumes, health, and anything else related to the now important fashion industry. The latest fashions appeared in automobile and travel advertisements and even made an appearance in industrial ads. An advertisement for Englebert Ballon, which manufactured tires, depicted a stylishly dressed woman cheerfully sitting on a rubber tire. In response to the trend, the covers of the stodgier women's publications, such as *Delineator* in the United States, became more stylish by the 1930s. About 1927 *Delineator* brought in *Vogue*'s leading female cover artist, Helen Dryden,* to produce a series of fashionable covers.

Many important posterists were drawn into the fashion world as opportunities expanded. Loupot produced one of his most impressive poster designs, "O Cap," in 1928 to promote a shampoo. It can be seen as a double image, showing both a full face and a profile view of a woman's head—a device later seen in Picasso's work. Cassandre also created many designs in fashion graphics when he moved to the United States and worked regularly as a cover artist for *Harper's Bazaar*.* In his own distinctive way, Cassandre produced covers that often only hinted at fashion through the use of symbols. In July 1939 he designed one of his more straightforward covers. Like most of his work, it has a timeless quality and can be considered fashionable today.

Political turmoil and the Great Depression greatly hindered fashion developments in the 1930s. Even the wealthy did not have money to spend as they had previously. However, one exciting development in fashion during this decade was Madeleine Vionnet's bias-cut dress, which moved sensuously with a woman's body. (Escapist entertainment, such as the Hollywood movies, was a major psychological factor during this period, and women hungered for the dresses worn by the stars, featuring supple fabrics that

296

300

hugged the body and revealed the outline of the nipples.) The 1930s marked also the decline of the fashion illustrator, whose importance had begun to wane in the early part of the decade and was nearly nonexistent by the end. Illustrators were replaced by a new breed, the fashion photographers, such as Edward Steichen, George Hoyningen-Huene, and Cecil Beaton. Some photographs at first maintained a somewhat Deco look. A Bergdorf Goodman advertisement for a black crêpe dress with matching fox fur is a transitional piece from 1938, which attempted the characteristic geometric stylization using angled poses and a surrounding keyhole. Photography, however, did not lend itself to the transformation or distortion of reality that marked the Art Deco style. With the new medium, woman became not a creature of fantasy, but quite real.

275

RAWLINGS, *photograph for advertisement, 1938, U.S.A. (priv. coll.)*

BEFORE 1925

The watershed for Art Deco graphic design was 1925, with the great Paris Exposition marking the beginning of a new era—even though much of the innovation displayed dated back a decade or more. The change in fashion illustration was quite distinct, with exotic Orientalism having given way to a streamlined functionalism that produced the flat-chested "schoolboy" shape and the short-skirted, waistless tube worn by the flappers—a striking contrast with the wasp-waisted, full-bosomed, full-skirted styles of a generation before. Illustrators were influenced by Cubism and other new art styles as they interpreted the changing fashions.

PABLO PICASSO, *costume design for* Parade, *used for cover of Ballets Russes program, 1917, France*

NATALIA GONCHAROVA, *costume design, 1915, France (courtesy Sotheby's)*

ANONYMOUS, Les Idées Nouvelles de la Mode *magazine cover, 1924, France (priv. coll.)*

BAINS DE MER
VILLES D'EAUX

AU BON MARCHÉ
MAISON A. BOUCICAUT, PARIS

RENÉ VINCENT, *"Au Bon Marché," poster, c. 1925, France (Musée de l'Affiche, Paris)*

JANINE AGHION, **The Essence of the Mode of the Day,** *book illustration, 1920, France (Pat Kery Fine Arts, New York)*

G. BARBIER 1914

Sheherazade

*Maintenant, ô Sheherazade, que, pour la mille-et-unième fois, vous avez charmé
la nuit du sultan attentif et fantasque.....*

GEORGE BARBIER, *"Schéhérazade," magazine illustration for* Modes et Manières d'Aujourd'hui, *1914,*
France (Bibliothèque Forney, Paris)

GEORGES LEPAPE, *"Le Miroir Rouge," magazine illustration for*
Feuillets d'Art, *1919, France (Jadis et Naguère, Paris)*

GEORGES LEPAPE, *"Spinelly," poster, 1914, France (Pat Kery Fine
Arts, New York)*

CHARLES MARTIN, *"De la Pomme aux Lèvres," magazine illustration for* la Gazette du Bon Ton, *c. 1915, France (Bibliothèque Forney, Paris)*

ANONYMOUS, *Gaut-Blancan et Cie. stationery design*, 1924–30, France (Bibliothèque Forney, Paris)

AUSTIN COOPER, *"Joliway to Holiday L.N.E.R.,"* poster, Great Britain (coll. Roger Coisman)

APRÈS LA DANSE

ROBE DE DINERS DE WORTH

ALEX POZERURISKI, *"Après la Danse," magazine illustration for* La Gazette du Bon Ton, *c. 1915,*
France (Bibliothèque Forney, Paris)

L. METLICOVITZ, *"Calzaturificio de Varese," postcard based on poster,
1914, Italy (priv. coll.)*

GEORGES LEPAPE, Vogue *magazine cover ("optical dress" by Sonia Delaunay), 1925, U.S.A. (priv. coll.)*

ADIEU, PAUVRE AMOUR...

ROBE D'APRÈS-MIDI EN "PALMES AGNELLA", DE RODIER

GEORGES LEPAPE, *"Adieu Pauvre Amour,"* magazine illustration for La Gazette du Bon Ton, *1921,*
France (priv. coll.)

289

LÉON BAKST, *costume design for ballet* La Légende de Joseph, *1922, France (courtesy Sotheby's)*

WALTER SCHNACKENBERG, *"Odeon Casino," poster, 1920, France (coll. Merrill C. Berman)*

1925 AND AFTER

ANONYMOUS, *"Happy New Year," greeting card, c. 1925, U.S.A. (Jadis et Naguère, Paris)*

SONIA DELAUNAY, *portfolio illustration, "Ses Peintures, Ses Objets, Ses Tissus Simultanés, Ses Modes,"*
c. 1925, France (Leonard Fox Rare Books, New York)

Exposition
de
ROBES
&
MANTEAUX

Samedi 23
Lundi 25
Mardi 26
OCTOBRE

MARC-LUC, *"Exposition de Robes et Manteaux," poster, c. 1928, France (Musée de l'Affiche, Paris)*

DYNEVOR RHYS, *"Garden Party Frock from Goupy," magazine illustration for* Harper's Bazaar, *April 1931, U.S.A. (Jadis et Naguère, Paris)*

294

RENÉ MAGRITTE, *"Primevère," poster, 1926, Belgium (Wolfgang Ketterer, Munich)*

E. G. BENITO, Vanity Fair *magazine cover, December 1930, U.S.A. (priv. coll.)*

ANONYMOUS, *poster, c. 1925, Japan (Shiseido Cosmetics, Tokyo)*

SONIA DELAUNAY, *portfolio illustration, "Ses Peintures, Ses Objets, Ses Tissus Simultanés, Ses Modes," c. 1925, France (Pat Kery Fine Arts, New York)*

HELEN DRYDEN, Delineator *magazine cover, March 1929, U.S.A. (priv. coll.)*

REYALDO LUZA, *portfolio illustration, "Révillon Frères," 1927–28. France (Leonard Fox Rare Books, New York)*

ANONYMOUS, *poster, c. 1925, Japan (Shiseido Cosmetics, Tokyo)*

E. G. BENITO, *portfolio illustration*, La Dernière Lettre Persane, *c. 1925, France (Leonard Fox Rare Books, New York)*

A. M. CASSANDRE, Harper's Bazaar *magazine cover, July 1939, U.S.A. (priv. coll.)*

VOGUE

INCORPORATING VANITY FAIR

HOT WEATHER
HOLIDAYS
JULY 1, 1938
PRICE 35¢

GEORGES LEPAPE, *Vogue magazine cover, July 1938, U.S.A. (priv. coll.)*

RENÉ VINCENT, *"Golf de Sarlabot,"* poster, 1930, France (Pat Kery/Jacques Mallet Fine Arts, New York)

Mars 1927

Prix: 6 frs.

femina

PREMIÈRES
ROBES
ET
TISSUS
PRINTANIERS

Mourgue. 27

PIERRE MOURGUE, Femina *magazine cover, March 1927, France (priv. coll.)*

VLADIMIR BOBRITSKY, Vanity Fair *magazine cover, October 1926, U.S.A. (priv. coll.)*

COL VAN HEUSEN

LE COL SEMI — DUR

CHARLES LOUPOT, *"Col. Van Heusen," poster, 1928, France (Jacques Mallet Fine Arts, New York)*

LEO MARFURT, *"Belga," poster and advertisement, 1935, Belgium*
(Pat Kery Fine Arts, New York)

PIERRE MOURGUE, Vogue *magazine cover, March 16, 1929, U.S.A.*
(priv. coll.)

LÉO MARFURT, "Ostende-Douvres," poster, c. 1928, Belgium (Eric Leyton, New York)

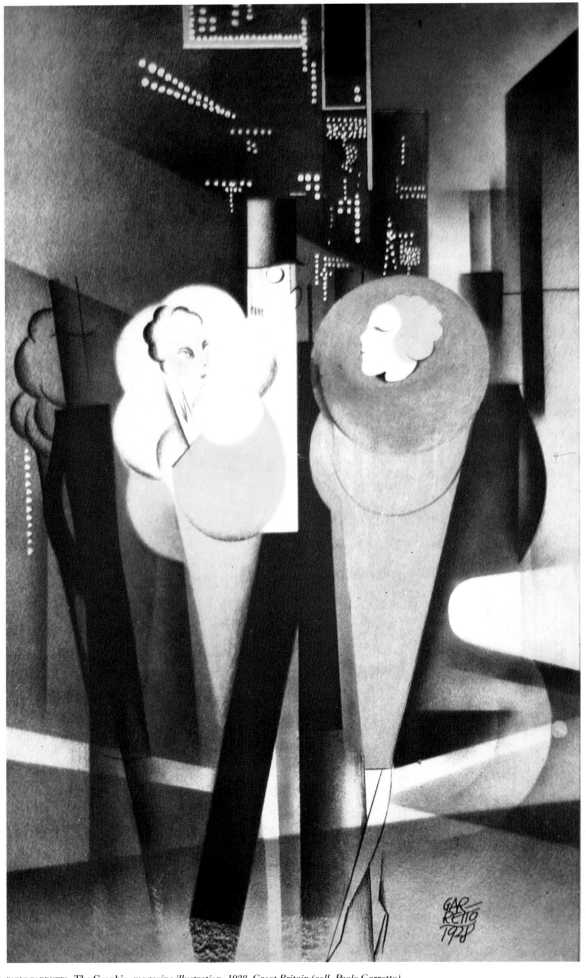

PAOLO GARRETTO, **The Graphic**, *magazine illustration, 1928, Great Britain (coll. Paolo Garretto)*

Biographical notes

Some biographical information about designers and illustrators whose works appear in this book. Omitted, with a few special exceptions, are well-known painters and other artists who have done some graphic works but are not primarily graphic artists.

AGHION, JANINE (b. France, 1894). Designer, graphic artist, book illustrator. Began her career designing for Poiret in the Atelier Martine. Illustrated limited-edition albums and fashion magazines in the 1920s.

ALASTAIR (Hans Henning Voigt) (b. Germany, 1887). Book illustrator. Self-taught as an artist; influenced by Aubrey Beardsley. *Forty-three Drawings by Alastair* published in 1914. Did many book illustrations in the 1920s. One-man exhibition in New York (Weyhe Gallery, 1925). After 1930s stopped drawing altogether.

ALEXEIEFF, ALEXANDER (b. Russia, 1901–d. 1982). Decorator, graphic artist, designer, posterist. Studied at Institute of Oriental Languages, Paris. 1922–25: designed stage sets, costumes, show posters. Late 1920s: lithographer, wood engraver, etcher (especially for book illustrations). Best known for innovations in film animation.

ARMITAGE, MERLE (b. 1893–d. 1975). American book designer, publisher; helped modernize American book design. Promoted new graphic arts ideas. Art director, *Look* magazine.

ARPKE, OTTO (b. Germany, 1886–d. 1943). Painter, graphic artist, lithographer, posterist, mainly in Berlin. Later, taught commercial art in Berlin, arts and crafts in Mainz.

BAKST, LÉON (Léon Rosenberg) (b. Russia, 1868–d. 1924). Painter, set, textile, and costume designer; illustrator; graduate of Imperial Academy of Arts, St. Petersburg. 1893–96: studied with Albert Edelfelt in Paris. C. 1900 returned to St. Petersburg and joined the Mir Iskusstva (The World of Art), avant-garde art movement that published an art magazine by that name; both led in part by Diaghilev. Joined Diaghilev in Paris in 1909, designing sets and costumes for the Ballets Russes. First London exhibition in 1912 (Fine Art Society).

BARBIER, GEORGE (b. France, 1882–d. 1932). (Barbier spelled "George" without the "s" customary in the French form.) Graphic artist, painter, set designer, fashion and book illustrator; also designed textiles, wallpaper, posters, packaging, postcards, and stage and cinema costumes and sets, with particular interest in dance. The Ballets Russes inspired his first illustrated albums, *Nijinsky* and *Karsavina*.

BAUGNIET, MARCEL LOUIS (b. Belgium, 1896). Painter, printmaker, graphic artist; studied at Académie des Beaux-Arts, Brussels. 1922–29: joined the group "7 Arts" and did advertising and decorative work. Designed posters, ads, furniture; worked in typography, etching, lithography, wood engraving. 1972: founded (with Jean Milo) the movement "Coll'Art." Numerous shows in Europe and the U.S. after 1921.

BAUMBERGER, OTTO (b. Switzerland, 1889–d. 1961). Designer, lithographer, posterist; schooled in Munich, Paris, London, but worked mostly in Zurich. Helped establish the Swiss School of Graphic Design early in the century. Employed as lithographer at J. E. Wolfensberger; became a partner in 1914. 1916–18: produced theater posters. After the war he became active in stage design, and by 1920 was designing sets for theaters in Berlin and Zurich. 1920–59: professor of art in Zurich.

BAYER, HERBERT (b. Austria, 1900–d. 1985). Typographer, painter, designer, photographer. 1920: worked with architect Emanuel Mangold. 1921: studied at Bauhaus, Weimar. 1925–28: taught advertising layout, typography at Bauhaus, Dessau. 1928–38: worked in Berlin as comercial artist, typographer, exhibition designer, photographer, painter. Went to the U.S. in late 1930s; worked as

a graphic artist for *Fortune* magazine, Container Corporation of America, many others.

BEGGARSTAFF BROTHERS: JAMES PRYDE (b. Scotland, 1869–d. 1941), WILLIAM NICHOLSON (b. England, 1872–d. 1949). Graphic artists, painters, posterists, theater designers. Pryde studied at the Royal Scottish Academy of the Arts and Académie Julian, Paris. Nicholson studied briefly at Académie Julian and enrolled at Sir Hubert von Herkomer's School, Bushey, England, but was mostly self-taught. In 1893 he married Pryde's sister and began collaboration with Pryde; successful aesthetically but not commercially. As of 1899, each worked independently in painting, printmaking, and theater design.

BEHRENS, PETER (b. Germany, 1868–d. 1940). Architect, painter, designer; studied in Karlsruhe and Dusseldorf, then traveled to Netherlands and Italy. 1890s: designed book bindings, prints, posters in the Art Nouveau style. 1898: designed flacons for a glass factory; credited with inventing what is now named industrial design. 1899: participated in Die Sieben group in Darmstadt. 1901: first architectural project. From c. 1900, a major proponent of functional style, which became fully realized with the Bauhaus teachings from 1919. 1903: appointed director of Dusseldorf School of Arts and Crafts. 1907: director of design for the AEG conglomerate, designing products, packaging, publicity, exhibitions, stores, offices, factories, and buildings. Pioneer of modern architecture in Germany, aligned with Mackintosh and Van de Velde. Influenced a generation of architects, including Gropius, Le Corbusier, Mies van der Rohe.

BELLENGER, PIERRE (b. France, 1909–). Painter, posterist, graphic artist. Established reputation 1929: won first prize for poster, Exposition d'Organisation Commerciale, Paris. 1935: exhibited at Salon d'Automne. Designed many posters with his twin brother, Jacques (often signing "J. P. Bellenger"), and maintained studio with him c. 1936–77. 1985: designed stamp for France.

BENEDICTUS, ÉDOUARD (b. France, 1878–d. 1930). Painter, bookbinder, fabric designer, created albums of decorative abstract Art Deco motifs.

BENITO, EDUARDO GARCIA (b. Spain, 1891). Painter and graphic artist; studied in Valladolid, at Belles Artes de San Fernando, Madrid, École des Beaux Arts, Paris. From c. 1919 lived in Paris and New York, illustrating books and fashion magazines. From 1921, for about two decades was a leading cover artist for international editions of *Vogue*. Became a portrait painter and muralist.

BERNHARD, LUCIEN (b. Austria, 1883–d. 1972). Posterist, typographer, graphic artist, architect; studied at Munich Academy but self-taught as designer and architect. Designed furniture, rugs, wallpaper, lighting fixtures, as well as office buildings, factories, and houses. 1923: settled in the U.S., working as interior designer and teaching graphic arts. Maintained Bernhard-Rosen studio in Berlin. Cofounder of the international design firm Contempora (with Rockwell Kent, Paul Poiret, Bruno Paul).

BINDER, JOSEPH (b. Austria, 1898–d. 1972). Graphic artist, designer, painter, posterist; studied at School of Arts and Crafts, Vienna. 1924: established studio in Vienna. 1925–29: designed posters and packaging for coffee and tea importer. 1933–35: taught graphic design in the U.S. 1935: became free-lance artist and graphic designer in New York; continued lecturing and teaching. 1939: created official poster for New York World's Fair.

BIRNBAUM, ABE (b. 1899). American cartoonist, illustrator; studied at the Art Students League. Cartoonist for

The New Yorker in the 1940s and '50s. Drew for *Harper's Bazaar* and other publications. Exhibited at the 1939 World's Fair, New York. 1945: illustrated *Listen to the Mocking Words*.

BOBRITSKY, VLADIMIR V. (b. Ukraine, 1898–). Set designer, graphic artist, book and magazine illustrator, muralist, musician, painter; attended the Imperial Art School and designed sets for the Great Dramatic Theater, Kharkov. Forced off to war in the Ukraine; fled to America in 1921 and operated textile firm. Prolific in advertising, specializing in fashion-oriented products and fashion magazine covers. Directed radio programs and wrote several books about music. Also signed "Bobri."

BRODOVITCH, ALEXEY (b. Russia, 1900–d. 1971). Designer, posterist, graphic artist, editorial designer. 1917: went to France. 1920: worked for Diaghilev as painter. 1924: designed posters. 1928: artistic director for Trois Quartiers and Madelios. 1934–58: artistic director of *Harper's Bazaar*. During 1940s and '50s, taught editorial design classes at New School for Social Research, New York. 1948: director of *Portfolio* magazine.

CAPPIELLO, LEONETTO (b. Italy, 1875–d. 1942). Painter, designer, caricaturist, posterist. 1898: settled in Paris, where he designed posters for four decades. Began career as a caricaturist, contributed to *Le Rire*, *L'Assiette au Beurre*, others. 1899: his first poster created a sensation, and he went on to publish thousands more.

CARLU, JEAN (b. France, 1900–d. 1983). Designer and posterist. Studied architecture originally but became a posterist after World War I. Active in all the graphic arts, but mostly designed posters. From 1932, he became involved in political causes, and in the late 1930s and the '40s designed posters in the U.S. He wrote articles and lectured on his theories. Returned to France after the war.

CASSANDRE, A. M. (Adolphe Mouron) (b. Russia, 1901–d. 1968). Painter, posterist, theater designer, typographer; studied at the Académie Julian, Paris. 1923: designed his first poster. 1925: won first prize for posters, Paris Exposition. 1926: founded the Alliance Graphique with Maurice Moyrand. 1936: exhibition at Museum of Modern Art, New York. 1936–39: worked in the U.S., designed covers for *Harper's Bazaar*. 1939: returned to France and almost completely abandoned posters in favor of advertising, theatrical design, painting.

CHIMOT, ÉDOUARD (b. France, 1880–d. 1949). Engraver, designer, book illustrator; studied in Nice, then Paris. Illustrated many books, such as *Le Spleen de Paris* by Baudelaire. Prolific engraver.

COLIN, PAUL (b. France, 1892–d. 1985). Painter, posterist, costume and set designer. 1913: went to Paris. 1925: success of the *Revue Nègre*, which started his long association with Josephine Baker. Created more than a thousand posters and designed costumes and stage sets for the Paris Opera, other theaters. 1926: opened a school for graphic art.

COOPER, AUSTIN (b. Canada, 1890–d. 1964). Painter, posterist; studied at Cardiff School of Art, Abroath, City and Guilds School, Kensington. After working briefly in Canada, moved to London in 1922, designing posters for London and North Eastern Railway (L.N.E.R.), London Underground, others. 1938–40: principal of Reimann School of Industrial Art. 1943: turned to painting. 1948: first one-man show in London.

COULON, ERIC DE (b. Neuchâtel, 1888). Swiss posterist; studied architecture at Polytechnical School, Zurich. 1910–12: studied under L'Eplattenier, began to design furniture and wood sculpture. 1913: went to Paris, did advertising design. 1918: founded advertising agency. 1917: his first posters commissioned by Galeries Lafayette. Designed advertisements for department stores. Primarily a posterist, but also did window displays, packaging, decoupage.

COVARRUBIAS, MIGUEL (b. Mexico, 1904–d. 1957). Caricaturist, graphic artist, designer, writer, anthropologist. 1923: arrived in New York with little formal training. Became in less than three years one of America's most acclaimed caricaturists, published in *Vanity Fair, Vogue, The New Yorker*. 1925: illustrated *The Prince of Wales and Other Famous Americans*. In the 1930s he pursued a second career in anthropology, but continued drawing. Also did textile design, window displays, advertising.

CSAKY, JOSEPH (b. Hungary, 1888–d. 1971). Sculptor; studied briefly at Budapest Academy of Applied Arts. 1908: went to Paris. 1911: exhibited at the Salon d'Automne and Salon des Indépendants. He was among the earliest to construct figures of cones, cylinders, and spheres. Cubism was the dominant idiom of his work. After 1935 it was modified by classical tendencies.

CZESCHKA, CARL OTTO (b. Austria, 1878–d. 1960). Graphic artist, designer, book illustrator. Studied in Vienna under Kokoschka. Member of Vienna Secession, designer for Wiener Werkstätte, professor at the School of Arts and Crafts until 1970. Went to Hamburg, where he continued to design in the Secession style. Did book illustrations, graphic art, designed theater sets, costumes, furniture, jewelry, silverware, metalwork. Also known for his work in Max Reinhardt's Deutsches Theater, Berlin, and the Palais Stoclet, Brussels. C. 1915: designed cigar packaging and labels in Hamburg for the L. Wolff Company.

DELAMARE, FRANCIS. Belgian posterist, graphic artist. Created first posters around 1916. 1920s: cofounded advertising agency. 1930: exhibited posters at the Exposition Internationale de l'Affiche Contemporaine, Liège.

D'ALBISOLA, TULLIO (Tullio Mazotti) (b. Italy, 1899–d. 1971). Poet, ceramicist, photographer, sculptor. Became part of Futurist group in Savone. 1930s: instrumental in publishing the first Futurist books bound in tin.

DEFFKE, WILHELM (b. Germany–d. 1950). Graphic designer. 1920s: had own studio in Berlin. Designed trademarks, posters, other graphic work for corporations, publishing houses. Later became director of Magdeburg Arts and Crafts School.

DOMERGUE, JEAN-GABRIEL (b. France, 1889–d. 1964). Painter, graphic artist; studied at École des Beaux Arts. 1913: won Prix de Rome. Produced portraits of celebrities and society women. Occasionally designed posters. Illustrated several books.

DRYDEN, HELEN (b. U.S.A., 1887–d. 1934). Graphic artist, posterist, painter, set designer; attended Pennsylvania Academy of Fine Arts. Leading female cover illustrator of international editions of *Vogue* in 1910s and '20s. Also worked for *Delineator* and other American publications. 1915: won a prize in Newark Poster Competition. C. 1930: art director, Dura Co., Toledo, Ohio. 1938–39: industrial designer of automobiles, considered her most important work. Also did fabric design, stage sets, packaging, and painted portraits.

DUDOVICH, MARCELLO (b. Trieste, 1878–d. 1962). Painter, graphic artist, posterist. 1895: did graphics for Ricordi. 1899: worked in Bologna. 1900: received gold medal for Paris Exposition Universelle poster. After long sojourn in Munich, went to Milan. Contributed illustrations to *Novovissima, Rapidista, Ars et Labor*, and *Simplicissimus* until 1911. Considered one of the greatest Italian poster artists.

DUPAS, JEAN-BORDEAUX (b. France, 1882–d. 1964). Painter, graphic artist, posterist; studied at Bordeaux and Écoles des Beaux Arts, Paris. 1910: awarded First Grand Prix de Rome and studied under Carolus Duran and Albert Bernard. Besides mural and easel painting, designed posters, illustrated books, periodicals, brochures. Also executed large compositions on glass for ocean liners. 1942–52: taught painting at École des Beaux Arts.

DWIGGINS, W. A. (William Addison) (b. U.S.A., 1880–d. 1956). Graphic artist, typographer; studied with Goudy at turn of century. Designed hundreds of books for Alfred A. Knopf. 1920s: coined the term "graphic designer" to describe his activities. Designed Electra type and others. 1938: produced Caledonia, one of the most widely used typefaces in America. Designed marionettes, puppets, and marionette theaters.

EDEL, EDMUND (b. Germany, 1863–d. 1933). Painter, graphic artist, advertiser, writer; studied in Munich and Paris. Worked in Berlin from 1892. After 1897, became one of the best-known German poster artists.

ENGELHARD, JULIUS USSY (b. Sumatra, 1883–d. 1964). Painter, posterist, graphic artist; studied at Munich Academy. Before and after World War I, one of the best-known German posterists. Contributed to many German sporting papers, fashion magazines, and *Simplicissimus*. Member, New Munich Association of Poster Artists.

ERDT, HANS RUDI (b. Germany, 1883–d. 1918). Graphic artist, advertiser, lithographer; studied at Munich School of Decorative Arts. One of the best-known Berlin posterists after 1908.

ERTÉ (Romain de Tirtoff) (b. Russia, 1892–). Painter, stage, costume, and fashion designer, ilustrator; studied painting at Académie Julian, Paris. 1913: designer for Poiret. 1914: moved to Monte Carlo, produced covers, fashion illustrations, and regular illustrated columns for *Harper's Bazaar*. Designed costumes and sets for theaters, nightclubs, revues, and films. Achieved renown c. 1925 for scenery and costumes for Folies-Bergère. 1929–30: produced fabrics and dresses for Amalgamated Silk Corp., New York. Continued to design for theater, opera, music halls, film, advertising, magazine and book illustration. Major resurgence of fame in 1960s.

FEININGER, LYONEL (b. U.S.A., 1871–d. 1956). Painter, graphic artist; studied at Arts and Crafts School, Hamburg, Berlin Academy. 1892–1906: magazine illustrator and cartoonist. 1906–1908: devoted himself to painting. 1913: exhibited in Berlin with the Blaue Reiter group. 1919–33: taught at Bauhaus, Weimar and Dessau. 1924: founded group of "Blue Four" with Kandinsky, Klee, and Jawlensky. 1937: settled in New York. Exhibited in Germany and the U.S.

FENNECKER, JOSEF (b. Germany, 1895–d. 1956). Painter, graphic artist, stage designer; studied in Dusseldorf, Munich, Berlin. From 1918, one of the leading cinema poster artists in Berlin.

FISH (Anne Sefton) (b. England, 1892–d. 1964). Caricaturist, cartoonist, graphic artist; studied at London School of Art and in Paris. 1913: designed textiles. 1914: began contributing satirical drawings to the *Tatler* and *Vanity Fair*. Contributed to many magazines, including *Printer's Pie, Cosmopolitan, Harper's Bazaar, Pan*, and *Punch*. Illustrated about ten books.

GARRETTO, PAOLO (b. Italy, 1903–). Caricaturist, painter, graphic artist; studied at Accademia di Belle Arti, Milan. One of the most international magazine cover artists of the period. 1926: went to London, contributed to *Tatler, Vogue, La Rivista, Le Rire, Fantasia, The New Yorker, Natura*, others. 1931: went to New York, contributed to *Vanity Fair, Vogue, Harper's Bazaar, Town and Country, Fortune*. 1942: returned to Italy, did illustration for *Bellazza, Arbiter*. Also designed stage sets, costumes, theater publications, and was involved in cartoon animation.

GESMAR, CHARLES (b. France, 1900–d. 1928). Posterist, set and costume designer. His first surviving poster dates from 1916. Later worked for Folies-Bergère and Olympia Music Hall. C. 1917, became constant companion of Mistinguett. Designed her extravagant costumes, stage sets, program covers for Casino de Paris and Moulin Rouge. His vibrant, witty style would always be identified with the French music hall.

GILL, ERIC (b. England, 1882–d. 1940). Sculptor, engraver, typographer, writer; studied at Chichester Art School, Central School of Arts and Crafts. 1903: became independent letter cutter and monument mason. 1910–19: went to Ditchling, Sussex, and did his first printing for St. Dominic's Press of Pepler. 1924: moved to Capel-y-Fin in Wales, worked for Golden Cockerel Press. 1925: designed type for Monotype Corporation. 1920: moved to Pigotts at Speen, established own press, and worked in the firm of Hague and Gill, printers. Did stone masonry, inscription carving, typeface design, lettering, graphic design, advertising, and extensive writing.

GIPKINS, JULIUS (b. Germany, 1883). Graphic artist, poster artist, designer; self-taught. One of best-known poster artists. Also designed window displays, lighting fixtures, furniture, interior furnishings, packaging.

GRONOWSKI, TADEUS (b. Poland, 1894). Posterist and designer; studied at School of Architecture, Polytechnical School, Warsaw, and École des Beaux Arts, Paris. He was the first professional Polish poster artist. Also did

book and magazine covers, typographical compositions, labels, pamphlets, postage stamps, theater sets, murals, furniture. Coeditor of *Grafika*. Awarded many prizes in international competitions.

HELD, JOHN, JR. (b. U.S.A., 1889–d. 1958). Graphic artist, cartoonist, sculptor, ceramicist; studied with Mahonri Young. Began career as newspaper sports cartoonist. 1910: moved to New York, illustrated newspapers and advertising, then magazines. In the 1920s and '30s his stylized flapper was seen often in major magazines. His cartoon strips "Margie and Ra" and "Ra Rosalie" were popular in the 1930s. Did sculpture and ceramics in later years. Artist-in-residence at Harvard University, University of Georgia.

HERDIG, WALTER (b. Switzerland, 1908–). Graphic artist, publisher. Collaborated on unified campaign for St. Moritz, from letterheads to posters. Publisher of *Graphis* magazine.

HOFFMANN, JOSEF (b. Austria, 1870–d. 1956). Architect, textile designer, graphic artist, craftsman; studied at the Vienna Academy with Wagner. Founding member, Vienna Secession. 1899–1941: professor at Vienna School of Arts and Crafts. 1903: a founder of the Wiener Werkstätte. 1912: founded Austrian Craft Society.

HOHLWEIN, LUDWIG (b. Germany, 1874–d. 1949). Posterist, architect, graphic artist; studied architecture at Munich Technical College, no formal training in the graphic arts. 1906: devoted himself primarily to poster design. His unique contributions were his unified concept, using every element in the poster to create a single effect, and techniques for applying color. He belonged to no school or group. He designed numerous advertisements and Nazi propaganda posters.

ICART, LOUIS (b. France, 1880–d. 1950). Painter, printmaker; no formal training. 1907: arrived in Paris, worked for postcard company. By 1908 had his own studio; progressed from postcards to magazines and fashion design. 1916: contributed to *Le Rire, Fantasia, La Baïonette*. From 1918 he devoted himself mostly to etching and painting. Developed extreme skill as etcher, using complex mixture of techniques. His sensuous, romantic, sophisticated heroine became one of the symbols of the Art Deco woman. He illustrated many limited-edition books.

IRIBE, PAUL (b. France, 1883–d. 1935). Painter, designer; studied at Collège Rollin and the École Condorcet, Paris. 1898–99: apprenticed in typography at *Le Temps*. Contributed cartoons and illustrations to *L'Assiette au Beurre* and other publications. 1908: founded *Le Témoin*. Illustrated the first modern album of fashion plates for Poiret. Produced many fashion-related illustrations c. 1912. Set up studio, designed furniture, fabrics, wallpaper, and objets d'art. 1914: went to U.S., worked as designer for Cecil B. De Mille, others. Returned to France in late 1920s, and illustrated books, periodicals, and costume jewelry for his close friend Chanel.

JUNGE, CARL STEPHEN (b. U.S.A., 1880). Designer, painter, illustrator; studied at Hopkins Art Institute, London School of Art, and Académie Julian, Paris. Designer of Art Deco covers for *Inland Printer* magazine c. 1916, changing from his early Art Nouveau style, and book illustrator. He worked in California.

KANDINSKY, WASSILY (b. Russia, 1866–d. 1944). Painter, graphic artist, writer; studied painting in Munich. 1901: cofounded exhibiting association "Phalanx." 1911: created first abstract painting. 1911: cofounded the Blaue Reiter group. At the beginning of the war he returned to Russia, but his conception of art as spiritual process conflicted with the utilitarian doctrine of Constructivists. 1921: left to teach at the Bauhaus, where he stayed until its closing. 1933: settled in Paris.

KEIMEL, HERMANN (b. Germany, 1889). Painter, graphic artist, posterist; studied at Munich Academy. Professor at School of German Painting, Munich. Member of the Munich artists' group "The Twelve" and the New Munich Association of Poster Artists. Large graphic production. Instructor at the master-school for German handwork in Munich.

KENT, ROCKWELL (b. U.S.A., 1882–d. 1971). Painter, graphic artist, architect, book illustrator; studied architecture at Columbia University. Important American book illustrator; also distinguished as designer of book jackets, bookplates, and national ad campaigns. Commissioned to do murals for the U.S. Post Office and the Federal Building, Washington. He wrote three autobiographical works, including *It's Me, O Lord* (1955).

KLINGER, JULIUS (b. Austria, 1876–d. 1950). Painter, graphic artist, posterist; studied in Vienna. Associated with the Vienna Secession. Moved to Berlin and in 1897 illustrated comic magazines. After 1900, well-known Berlin poster artist. From the beginning of World War I, he worked in Vienna, where he later had his own studio.

LAAN, KEES VAN DER (b. Netherlands, 1903). Posterist. Worked in the Netherlands. Specialized in travel posters during the 1930s.

LABORDE, CHARLES (b. Argentina, 1886–d. 1941). Printmaker, book illustrator; studied at Académie Julian and École des Beaux Arts, Paris. Contributed to Parisian humor magazines from 1901. During World War I, did pictorial reportage from the front. After the war, devoted himself to book illustration.

LABOUREUR, JEAN-ÉMILE (b. France, 1877–d. 1943). Printmaker, book illustrator; studied at Académie Julian, Paris. 1912: exhibited at the Salon d'Automne. During the war, became a skilled engraver, best known for studies of British and American troops in World War I. 1923: founded the Société des Peintres-Graveurs Indépendants. Wrote articles on engraving. From 1920, devoted himself largely to book illustration.

LEBEDEV, VLADIMIR (b. 1891–d. 1964). Graphic artist. His first drawings were published in newspapers. 1920–22: with Kozlinsky, directed the Petrograd branch of ROSTA. Originated new concept of children's books.

LECK, BART VAN DER (b. Netherlands, 1876–d. 1958). Painter, posterist; studied at State School for Decorative Arts, Utrecht, and the Academy in Amsterdam. Produced very stylized paintings and posters. 1917: joined de Stijl group and further abstracted his subjects. Designed rugs, ceramics, and interior decoration.

LÉGER, FERNAND (b. France, 1881–d. 1955). Painter; studied at École des Arts Décoratifs and Académie Julian, Paris. Attracted to Cubism, Constructivism, and later to images of the machine. 1920: met and later worked with Le Corbusier, executing murals for the 1925 Paris Exposition. Active in experimental cinema, stage, and costume design, and produced magazine covers for *Fortune* (U.S.), *Cerpa* (Italy), *Gutenbergus* (Denmark), and others. During World War II, taught at Yale University and Mills College, California. 1945: returned to France. Executed projects for public buildings, mosaics, windows, tapestries, murals.

LEPAPE, GEORGES (b. France, 1887–d. 1971). Painter, posterist, fashion designer, book and magazine illustrator; studied at the Ateliers Humbert and Cormon, École Nationale des Beaux Arts, Paris. 1910: met Poiret, became active in fashion design, advertising, and graphics. 1911: illustrated *Les Choses de Paul Poiret*, which brought him international recognition. 1912: produced program illustrations for the Ballets Russes. Became one of the first Art Deco fashion illustrators. Executed countless covers and fashion illustrations for *Vogue* and *La Gazette du Bon Ton*. From 1920s, for thirty years worked regularly for *Harper's Bazaar*, *Femina*, *House and Garden*, *L'Illustration*, *Lu*, and *Vu*. Later he turned to book illustration and painting. Also designed advertising, brochures, sets and costumes.

LEWIS, (PERCY) WYNDHAM (b. Canada, 1882–d. 1957). Painter, novelist, critic; studied at Slade School. 1909: settled in England. 1913: joined the Omega Workshops, but broke away four months later. Founded Rebel Art Center, out of which came Vorticist movement. 1921: had solo exhibition and founded several art reviews, including *The Tyro*, *Blast*, and *The Enemy*. 1920s: wrote major books. Also did experimental drawings and portraits. 1939–45: went to Buffalo, New York, and Toronto. 1945: returned to England and became art critic for the *Listener*. He was among the first European artists to produce abstract paintings and drawings.

LEYENDECKER, J. C. (Joseph Christian) (b. Germany, 1874–d. 1951). Illustrator; attended Art Institute of Chicago, Académie Julian, Paris. Late 1890s: designed several covers in Art Nouveau style for *Inland Printer* magazine. 1898: opened studio in Chicago. 1899: designed first of 322 covers for *Saturday Evening Post* (continuing to 1943). 1900: moved to New York. 1905–30: created Arrow Shirt Collar Man advertisements. Designed propaganda posters for both World Wars.

EL (Eleazar) LISSITZKY (b. Russia, 1890–d. 1941). Painter, graphic artist, engineer, architect, theater designer, typographer; studied architecture in Darmstadt. 1915: started career as architect, graphic designer, painter. 1919: professor of architecture and graphics at the School of Fine Arts, Vitebsk. Became a major exponent of international Constructivism. Also did typographical design. 1922: went to Berlin, designed an exhibition that exposed Russian art to the West for the first time. With Moholy-Nagy and Gropius, had strong influence on Bauhaus design. 1928: returned to Russia, devoted himself to typography and exhibition design.

LÖFFLER, BERTHOLD (b. Bohemia, 1874–d. 1960). Studied at Vienna School of Arts and Crafts. 1905: cofounded the Vienna Ceramics workshop. 1907: took over Czeschka's class at the School of Arts and Crafts. 1912: exhibited at Rome International Exhibition.

LOUPOT, CHARLES (b. France, 1892–d. 1962). Graphic artist, posterist; studied at École des Beaux Arts, Lyon. 1916–23: did lithography and poster design in Switzerland. Moved to Paris, worked for *La Gazette du Bon Ton* and *Femina*, and designed advertisements. Created two posters for Voisin automobiles, one of which set the highly stylized direction he would pursue. 1930: joined Cassandre and Moyrand in their Alliance Graphique and exhibited his posters with Cassandre at Salle Pleyel. Illustrated and designed covers for many publications and continued as a leading poster artist after World War II.

LUZA, REYALDO (b. Peru, 1893). Painter, designer; studied in New York and made his reputation in Paris. Designed advertising illustrations. 1928: illustrated fashion portfolio of furs.

MACDONALD, MARGARET (b. 1865–d. 1933), **FRANCES MACDONALD** (b. 1874–d. 1921), **HERBERT MCNAIR** (b. 1868–d. 1955). Scottish designers. Sisters Margaret and Frances MacDonald met Charles Rennie Mackintosh and colleague Herbert McNair while studying at the Glasgow School of Art, and in 1893 they joined forces to become the "Glasgow Four." They designed posters, book illustrations, metalwork, and furniture. They participated in the 1900 exhibition in Vienna, contributing to the evolution of the Secessionist style.

MACKINTOSH, CHARLES RENNIE (b. Scotland, 1868–d. 1928). Designer, architect; apprenticed with a Glasgow architect, then worked as a draftsman. 1890s: worked with Margaret and Frances MacDonald and Herbert McNair to develop a distinctive style (Glasgow Art Nouveau). He designed the Glasgow School of Art, completed in 1909. His approach to architecture included furniture and interior design. 1914: settled in England.

MAN RAY (b. U.S.A., 1890–d. 1977). Painter, draftsman, sculptor, photographer; studied painting at Ferrer Center and other New York schools. About 1915 became involved in photography through Alfred Stieglitz. Founded New York Dada movement with Duchamp and Picabia. 1921: went to Paris, became prominent figure in Dada group and Surrealist movement. Regarded as one of the most innovative photographers of his time, especially noted for pioneering the photogram (rayograph) and the technique of solarization without using a camera. Known also for his abstract and surrealistic films, such as *Ewak Bakia* (1927). 1940: returned to U.S., settled in Hollywood. 1950: returned to Paris.

MARFURT, LÉO (b. Switzerland, 1894–d. 1977). Designer, posterist; studied at Aarau School of Arts and Crafts. 1910–14: printing apprenticeship. Assisted Jules de Praetere in his advertising studio. Studied graphics and painting at Geneva School of Fine Arts. 1921: returned to Belgium. 1923: started fifty-year association with tobacco firm, Vander Elst. Did advertising, packaging, and posters. Worked for other firms also. 1927: founded own advertising agency, Les Créations Publicitaires. Played a major role in reviving Belgian poster art.

MARTIN, CHARLES (b. France, 1884–d. 1934). Graphic artist, designer, fashion illustrator; studied at Montpelier École des Beaux Arts, Académie Julian, and École des Beaux Arts, Paris. Worked for *La Gazette du Bon Ton*, *Femina*, *Le Rire*, *Vogue*, *Harper's Bazaar*, others. Illustrated books, designed posters, sets and costumes, furniture, wallpaper, textiles, perfume bottles, fashions, panels and screens.

MARTY, ANDRÉ-ÉDOUARD (b. France, 1882–d. 1974). Painter, graphic artist, enameler; studied at École des Beaux Arts, Paris. Contributed to *La Gazette du Bon Ton*, *Femina*, *Vogue*, others. Also did etchings for books and designed theater sets and posters. Created designs that were executed in enamel on copper, vases, bowls, and jewelry.

MATTER, HERBERT (b. Switzerland, 1907–d. 1984). Graphic artist, designer, posterist, photographer; studied at École des Beaux Arts, Geneva, and Académie Moderne, Paris. 1928–29: worked with Cassandre on posters and Le Corbusier on architecture and exhibition design. 1930s: pioneered use of photography in graphic design and photomontage. 1932: returned to Switzerland, produced posters using these techniques. 1936: settled in New York. Did free-lance photography for *Harper's Bazaar* and *Vogue*, exhibition design for Museum of Modern Art. From 1940s, major contributor to Container Corporation ad campaigns. C. 1950: responsible for typography and book covers for Museum of Modern Art and Guggenheim Museum. Became professor of photography at Yale University and continued work as designer.

MAUZAN, LUCIEN-ACHILLE (b. France, 1883–d. 1952). Painter, graphic artist, posterist; studied at École des Beaux Arts, Lyon. 1905: began career in Italy, eventually producing over a thousand posters. 1927: went to Buenos Aires, where he continued to create posters at a frantic rate. 1933: returned to France. He was extremely prolific, producing thousands of postcards, paintings, sculptures, prints, and caricatures.

MCINTOSH, FRANK (b. U.S.A., 1901). Illustrator, graphic artist. Designed most of the covers for *Asia* magazine, late 1920s–mid-1930s. Designed for American publications.

MCKNIGHT-KAUFFER, EDWARD (b. U.S.A., 1890–d. 1954). Graphic artist, posterist, illustrator, theater designer; studied at Mark Hopkins Institute, San Francisco, and Chicago Institute. 1914: settled in England. Early work influenced by Cubism and Vorticism. 1915: began twenty-five years of producing posters for the London Underground. Designed books. 1937: one-man show at Museum of Modern Art, New York. 1940: returned to the U.S.

MOHOLY-NAGY, LÁSZLÓ (b. Hungary, 1895–d. 1946). Painter, sculptor, photographer, stage designer, author; turned from law to painting. 1921: moved to Berlin, experimented with collage and photomontage. 1922: exhibited at Der Sturm Gallery. 1923–28: taught at Bauhaus, coedited Bauhaus publications. Did experimental films, theater, industrial design, photography, typography, painting, sculpture, stage design. 1935: moved to London, joined Constructivist group. 1937: emigrated to Chicago, became director of New Bauhaus and cofounded the Institute of Design. Recognized for pioneering artistic uses of light, movement, photography, and plastic materials.

MORACH, OTTO (b. Switzerland, 1887–d. 1973). Painter, designer, posterist; studied mathematics at University of Bern, painting in Paris, Munich, Dresden, Berlin. 1919–53: professor of painting at School of Applied Arts, Zurich. From 1953, painted and worked in graphic art, stained glass, mosaics, panels, murals, etc.

MORELL, JOSÉ (b. Spain, 1899–d. 1949). Posterist. Prolific in the 1930s and 1940s, especially for products such as Philco radios and Underwood typewriters. Created posters for expositions in Barcelona in 1933 and 1934.

MOSER, KOLOMAN (KOLO) (b. Austria, 1868–d. 1918). Painter, graphic artist, designer, craftsman; studied at Academy of Creative Arts, Vienna, and Vienna School of Arts and Crafts (where he taught in 1900–18). 1897–1905: founding member, Vienna Secession. 1903: cofounded the Wiener Werkstätte. 1905: member of Klimt's group.

MÜLLER, C. O. (b. Germany, 1901). Graphic artist. Late 1920s: produced cinema posters for Phoebus Palast, using photomontage and asymmetrical typography. Specialized in linocuts.

NIELSEN, KAY (b. Denmark, 1886–d. 1957). Book illustrator, costume and set designer, designer; studied in Paris. Book illustrations exhibited in Paris, London, New York. Known in Denmark for porcelain figures. 1936: went to U.S. and worked for Walt Disney.

NIZZOLI, MARCELLO (b. Italy, 1887–d. 1969). Architect, graphic artist. Practiced architecture and advertising art in the 1930s, adhering to the Futurist doctrine.

NOVO (Nello Voltolina) (b. Italy, 1908–d. 1944). Painter, graphic artist. Became part of Futurist group in Padua and participated in their exhibitions. Used his real name only for his paintings.

ORSI (b. 1889–d. 1947). Posterist. A prolific artist, producing over one thousand posters, including several for Josephine Baker and for the Grand Guignol.

PETRUCELLI, ANTONIO (Anthony) (b. U.S.A., 1907–). Illustrator, painter; studied at Master School of United Arts, New York. 1929: did prize-winning cover for *House Beautiful.* Later illustrated many books for Time-Life, covers, illustrations, maps for such magazines as *Fortune* and *Life*. 1928: won an international press exhibition award, Cologne. 1957: designed postage stamps for Steel Centenary. 1973: created award-winning medal for Franklin Mint. Also designed textiles.

PLANK, GEORGE WOLF. American illustrator. One of the earliest (1912) and most prolific of the *Vogue* cover illustrators using the Art Deco style. Had imagination and a strong sense of composition. Adept at pen-and-ink drawings.

ROLLER, ALFRED (b. Austria, 1864–d. 1935). Painter, graphic artist, scenery designer; studied at Academy of Creative Arts, Vienna. Taught at the Vienna School of Arts and Crafts from 1899. 1897–1905: a founder and member of the Vienna Secession.

SATOMI, MUNETSUGU (Muneji) (b. 1900). Posterist. 1922: left Japan and went to Paris. Worked for Les Six Jours, KLM, and various Japanese companies.

SAUVAGE, SYLVAIN (b. 1888–d. 1948). Book illustrator, printmaker. Born into family of architects. Concerned with harmonious interaction between typography, decoration, and illustration, he became his own editor. Later, director of L'École Étienne.

SCHLEMMER, OSKAR (b. Germany, 1888–d. 1943). Painter, stage designer, sculptor; studied at Academy of Fine Arts, Stuttgart. 1914: designed murals for Deutsche Werkebund exhibition, Cologne. 1915: exhibited at Sturm Gallery, Berlin. From 1920: taught at Bauhaus, Weimar and Dessau. Head of theatrical design department and wood and stone masonry workshop. 1925: built and managed Bauhaus stage at Dessau. 1928: did murals for Museum Folkwang, Essen. Taught in Breslau (1929–32) and Berlin (1932–33).

SCHMIDT, JOOST (b. Germany, 1893–d. 1948). Engraver, painter, sculptor; studied at academy in Weimar and at Bauhaus, Weimar. 1925–1933: taught at Bauhaus, Dessau, head of the sculpture department and later of commercial typography department. 1933: declared a cultural Bolshevik and lost his studio. 1945: professor at Academy of Fine Arts, Berlin.

SCHMIED, FRANÇOIS-LOUIS (b. Switzerland, 1873–d. 1941). Painter, engraver, printer, publisher; studied at Geneva School of Industrial Arts. Early 1900s: went to Paris, set up as wood engraver. First important work was adapting and engraving Jouve's illustrations for Kipling's *Jungle Books*, completed 1918. Considered the best wood engraver in Paris. 1923: began to do his own book illustration. Ruined by the Depression.

SCHNACKENBERG, WALTER (b. Germany, 1880–d. 1961). Painter, designer, illustrator, posterist, theater designer; studied at Knorr's School of Painting in Munich. 1905: work exhibited at Berlin Secession. 1908–09: lived in Paris. 1911: member of Luitpold group in Munich. Known for posters, costume designs for ballet and theater. Contributed to *Jugend* magazine. Later years devoted to painting.

SCHULPIG, KARL (b. Germany, 1884–d. 1948). Graphic artist. Lived in Berlin. Produced posters and trademarks.

SCHULZ-NEUDAMM (b. Germany, 1899). Designer, posterist. Staff designer for publicity at UFA, a major German film studio in operation 1917–37.

SCHWITTERS, KURT (b. Germany, 1887–d. 1948). Painter, sculptor, posterist, poet; studied at Dresden and Berlin Academies and the Technical College of Hanover. 1918: exhibited at Sturm Gallery, Berlin. After war, settled in Hanover, invented a Dada style (*Merz*). 1922: invited to Holland by Van Doesburg to campaign for Dada, collaborated on typographic design projects. 1929: worked under Gropius as a typographer. 1923–32: produced posters for and edited the magazine *Merz*. Created collages using urban refuse. Worked as graphic consultant for city of Hanover and established own advertising studio. 1937: emigrated to Oslo. 1949: fled to England.

SEGUY, E. A. Designer. A prolific artist whose career spanned Art Nouveau and Art Deco. Worked in France, making colorful designs, primarily floral, some of which were published in pochoir portfolios. 1901: published *Les Fleurs et Leurs Applications Décoratives*.

SILVER, ROSE (Lisa Rhana) (b. U.S.A., 1902–d. 1985). Painter, illustrator; studied in Paris, Vienna, and at Parsons Graduate School of Design, New York. From late 1920s did covers for *The New Yorker* and *Time*, illustrations for *Vanity Fair*, and other graphic work. 1940s: abandoned graphics for painting and sculpture.

STEICHEN, EDWARD J. (b. Luxembourg, 1879–d. 1973). Photographer, painter, designer. 1882: moved to U.S. 1902: apprentice at a printing company. 1902: cofounded the Photo-Secession. 1910: studied painting in Paris. 1923–38: operated a commercial studio, working primarily in New York and Paris. Chief photographer for Condé Nast. Produced promotion pieces for such companies as Stehli Silk. 1929: participated in "Film & Photo" exhibition, Stuttgart, establishing reputation as photographer. Instrumental in new documentary trend in photography in the 1930s. Photographed important people, often for *Life* magazine. Received numerous awards in photography.

STENBERG BROTHERS: VLADIMIR (b. Russia, 1899), GEORGII (b. Russia, 1900–d. 1933). Studied at Stroganov School, Moscow, and at Svomas. 1923: began working on film posters. 1923–25: associated with *Lef* magazine and (until 1931) worked on designs, sets, and costumes for Alexander Tairov's Chamber Theater. 1925: received gold medal at Paris Exposition. Exhibited stage designs and film posters in Soviet Union and abroad. After Georgii's death, Vladimir continued designing posters.

STEPANOVA, VARVARA (b. Russia, 1894–d. 1958). Painter, designer, graphic artist; studied at Art School, Kazan. 1912: moved to Moscow and attended Stroganov Art School. Important painter who designed textiles, theater sets, typography, posters. 1923: with Popova and Rodchenko, designed at the First State Textile Print Factory. Fervent supporter of nonobjective art. Wrote and illustrated "transrational" poetry.

STORRS, JOHN (b. U.S.A., 1885–d. 1956). Painter, sculptor, printmaker; studied at Académie Julian, Paris, Chicago Art Institute, and with Auguste Rodin. 1913, 1920: exhibited at Salon d'Automne. 1920: one-man show at Folsom Galleries, New York. 1929: executed tall metal sculpture for Chicago Board of Trade Building. 1931: changed style and returned to painting.

SUGIURA, HISUI (b. Japan, 1876–d. 1965). Graphic artist who produced posters, including one for the opening of the subway system between Ueno and Asakusa.

TADA, HOKUU (b. Japan, 1889–d. 1948). Graphic artist and posterist. Did exhibition and product posters, especially for Kirin Beer and Lemonade in the 1930s.

TEIGE, KAREL (b. Czechoslovakia, 1900–d. 1950). Studied philosophy and art history at Charles University, Prague. Designed many typographical posters in late 1920s. 1923–31: edited *Stavba* magazine. Influential spokesman for functionalism. 1930: lectured at Bauhaus, Dessau, on sociology and architecture.

TEN BROEK, WILLEM FREDERIK (b. Netherlands, 1905). Posterist. Influenced by Cassandre. Produced travel posters for Dutch companies, and for the *Normandie* in 1935.

TSCHICHOLD, JAN (b. Germany, 1902–d. 1974). Typographer, writer; studied calligraphy at Academy of Book Design, Leipzig. 1925: began influential writings on typography, in articles and books introducing principles of "new typography" to printers and artists. Was early to recognize importance of photography in advertising. 1926–33: taught at Munich School for Master Book Printers. 1933: emigrated to Switzerland. By 1935, had returned to more traditional typographic style. 1947: invited to England to redesign Penguin Books.

VÉGH, GUSTAV (b. Hungary, 1890). Painter, designer. Lived in Berlin and Paris. Painter who specialized in scenes of everyday life in Paris. Graphic work included book covers.

VERTÈS, MARCEL (b. Hungary, 1895–d. 1962). Painter, graphic artist. Established reputation as leading poster artist in Vienna in early 1920s. 1925: went to Paris, produced two albums of lithographs. Later executed book illustrations, paintings, murals. Produced very few posters in Paris. Moved to the U.S. in late 1930s, painted murals for stores, restaurants, private houses. 1952: won two Academy Awards for set and costume design for the film *Moulin Rouge*.

VILMOS, HUSZAR (b. Hungary, 1884–d. 1960). Graphic artist, designer; studied at School of Decorative Arts in Budapest and Munich. 1905: settled in Netherlands. Worked on graphic art and designs for stained glass windows. 1917–23: involved with Theo van Doesburg and dé Stijl. Later returned to figurative painting.

VINCENT, RENÉ (b. France, 1879–d. 1936). Posterist, graphic artist, designer, painter. Studied architecture at École des Beaux Arts. Became illustrator for *La Vie Parisienne*, *L'Illustration*, *Saturday Evening Post* and created posters for Bon Marché. 1905: illustrated his first book. From 1920, concentrated on posters, signed "René Vincent," "Rageot," or "Dufour"; known especially for fashion and automobile posters. Also designed vases, table service, clocks, etc., which were executed in ceramic. 1924: opened workshop at Sèvres.

WARD, LYND (b. U.S.A., 1905–d. 1985). Graphic artist, book author and illustrator, printmaker; studied fine arts at Teachers College, Columbia University, New York, and National Academy for Graphic Arts, Leipzig. 1927–77: worked as illustrator and graphic artist. Illustrated about a hundred books, adult and juvenile, many of which had no written text. Exhibited wood engravings in national print shows.

WELSH, WILLIAM P. (b. U.S.A., 1889). Graphic artist. Prolific illustrator of magazine advertisements and covers. Contributed covers to *Woman's Home Companion* c. 1929; illustrated the book *Chicago*.

WYDEVELD, HENDRIKUS T. (b. Netherlands, 1885). Architect. 1905: went to England to study works of Morris and Ruskin, worked for architectural firm, attended Lambeth School of Art. 1911–13: went to France, worked in Lille and Paris, for architect Cordonnier. 1914: returned to Netherlands, started own practice designing houses, theaters, shops, interiors, and working-class apartments. 1918: founded the magazine *Wendingen*, published until 1931. Became advocate of Amsterdam school opposed to the de Stijl group.

YAMANA, AYAO. Japanese magazine illustrator and graphic artist. 1930s: instrumental in creating the Shiseido cosmetics firm's Art Deco image in ads, posters and packaging.

ZERO (Hans Schleger) (b. Germany, 1899). Graphic artist. Created numerous company trademarks. Produced a poster for Shell.

ZWART, PIET (b. Netherlands, 1885–d. 1977). Photographer, designer, typographer; trained at Amsterdam and Delft. 1919: taught at Académie Rotterdam. Designed furniture and interiors. Worked as assistant to architect Jan Wils. Associated with de Stijl artists. 1921: did typography, exhibitions, package and industrial design, photography. 1921–29: designed ads for Nederlandsche Kabelfabriek.

Bibliography

BOOKS

Ades, Dawn. *The 20th Century Poster—Design of the Avant-Garde*. New York: Abbeville Press, 1984.

Arnason, H. H. *History of Modern Art*. London: Thames and Hudson, 1969. New York: Harry N. Abrams, 1969.

Arwas, Victor. *Art Deco*. New York: Harry N. Abrams, 1980.

Barnicoat, John. *A Concise History of Posters*. London: Thames and Hudson, 1972.

Barr, Alfred H., Jr. *Fantastic Art, Dada, Surrealism*. New York: Museum of Modern Art, 1947.

Battersby, Martin. *The Decorative Twenties*. New York: Walker and Co., 1969.

———. *Art Deco Fashion, French Designers 1908–1925*. London: Academy Editions, 1974.

Bayer, Herbert, *Bauhaus 1919–1928*, ed. Walter Gropius and Ise. London: Bailey Brothers and Swinfen, 1959. Boston: Branford, 1959.

———. *Herbert Bayer painter designer architect*. New York: Reinhold, 1967.

Belleguie, André. *Le Mouvement de l'Espace Typographique: Années 1920–1930*. Paris: Jacques Damase, 1984.

Berry, W. Turner, A. F. Johnson, and W. P. Jaspert. *The Encyclopaedia of Type Faces*. London: Blandford, 1958.

Bie, Oskar. *Schnackenberg: Kostume/Plakate und Dekorationen*. Munich: Musarion Verlag, 1922.

Bigelow, Marybelle S. *Fashion in History: Apparel in the Western World*. Minneapolis: Burgess Publishing Co., 1970.

Binder, Carla. *Joseph Binder*. Vienna: Anton Schroll, 1976.

Bojko, Szymon. *New Graphic Design in Revolutionary Russia*. London: Lund Humphries, 1972.

Booth-Clibborn, Edward, and Daniele Baroni. *The Language of Graphics*. New York: Harry N. Abrams, 1980.

Bortolotti, Nadine. *Gli Annitrenta: Arte et Cultura in Italia*. Milan: Gabriele Mazzotta, 1982.

Brattinga, Pieter, and Dick Dooijes. *A History of the Dutch Poster 1890–1960*. Amsterdam: Scheltema and Holkema, 1968.

Brown, Robert K., and Susan Reinhold. *The Poster Art of A.M. Cassandre*. New York: E. P. Dutton, 1979.

Brunhammer, Yvonne. *The Nineteen-Twenties Style*. London: Paul Hamlyn, 1959.

———. *Art Deco Style*. New York: St. Martin's Press, 1984.

Cleaver, James. *History of Graphic Arts*. New York: Greenwood Press, 1963.

Clouzot, Henri. *Papiers, Peints et Teintures Modernes*. Paris: Charles Massin, 1928.

Cox, Beverly J., and Denna Jones Anderson. *Miguel Covarrubias Caricatures*. Washington, D.C.: Smithsonian Institution Press, 1985.

Curci, Roberto. *Marcello Dudovich*. Trieste: Edizioni Lint, 1976.

Damase, Jacques, and Sonia Delaunay. *Sonia Delaunay, Rythmes et Couleurs*. Paris: Hermann, 1971.

Daval, Jean-Luc. *Avant-Garde Art, 1914–1939*. New York: Rizzoli International Publications, 1980.

Delhaye, Jean. *Art Deco Posters and Graphics*. New York: Rizzoli International Publications, 1977.

Derval, Paul. *Folies-Bergère*. New York: E. P. Dutton, 1955.

Elliott, David, ed. *Rodchenko and the Arts of Revolutionary Russia*. New York: Pantheon Books, 1979.

Elson, Robert T. *Time, Inc.: An International History of a Publishing Empire, 1923–1941*. New York: Atheneum, 1968.

Fern, Alan, and Mildred Constantine. *Word and Image*. New York: Museum of Modern Art, 1968.

Frenzel, H. K. *Ludwig Hohlwein*. Berlin: Phönix Ilustrationsdruck und Verlag, 1926.

Fry, Edward F. *Cubism*. London: Thames and Hudson, 1966. New York: Oxford University Press, 1978.

Gallo, Max. *The Poster in History*. New York: American Heritage Publishing Co., 1974.

Garman, Ed. *The Art of Raymond Jonson, Painter*. Albuquerque: University of New Mexico Press, 1976.

Garner, Philippe, ed. *Encyclopédie Visuelle des Arts Décoratifs, 1890–1940*. Paris: Bordas, 1981.

Gold, Arthur, and Robert Fizdale. *Misia: The Life of Misia Sert*. New York: Alfred A. Knopf, 1980.

Hamilton, George Heard. *Painting and Sculpture in Europe, 1880–1940*. London: Penguin Books, Pelican History of Art, 1967.

Harlow, Frederica T. *The Illustrations of George Barbier*. New York: Dover Publications, 1977.

Haworth-Booth, Mark. *E. McKnight-Kauffer: A Designer and His Public*. London: Gordon Fraser, 1974.

Hillier, Bevis. *Art Deco*. New York: E. P. Dutton, 1969.

———. *Posters*. New York: Stein and Day, 1969.

———. *The World of Art Deco*. New York: E. P. Dutton, 1971.

Holme, Bryan. *Advertising, Reflections of a Century*. New York: Viking Press, a Studio Book, 1982.

Hornung, Clarence P., and Fridolf Johnson. *Two Hundred Years of American Graphic Art*. New York: George Braziller, 1976.

Hughes, Robert. *The Shock of the New*. New York: Alfred A. Knopf, 1981.

Hutchinson, F. Harold. *London Transport Posters*. London: London Transport Board, 1963.

Jardí, Enric, and Ramon Manent. *El Cartellisme a Catalunya*. Barcelona: Edicions Destino, 1983.

Johnson, Fridolf, ed. *Rockwell Kent, an Anthology of His Works*. New York: Alfred A. Knopf, 1981.

Kery, Patricia Frantz. *Great Magazine Covers of the World*. New York: Abbeville Press, 1982.

Koschatzky, Walter, and Horst-Herbert Kossatz. *Ornamental Posters of the Vienna Secession*. London: Academy Editions, 1970.

Lancelotti, A. *Mauzan, Cartelloni Opere Varie*. Milan: Bestettie Tumminelli, n.d.

Laynam, Ruth. *Couture: An Illustrated History of the Great Paris Designers and Their Creations*. New York: Doubleday and Co., 1972.

Lee, Marshall, ed. *Books for Our Time*. New York: Oxford University Press, 1950.

Lepape, Claude, and Thierry Defert. *From the Ballets Russes to Vogue—The Art of Georges Lepape*. New York: Vendome Press, 1984.

Lieberman, William S., ed. *Art of the Twenties*. New York: Museum of Modern Art, 1979.

Lista, Giovanni. *Le Livre Futuriste*. Modena: Edizioni Panini, 1984.

Loyer, Jacqueline. *Laboureur: Oeuvre Gravée et Lithographie*. Paris, 1962.

Lusk, Irène Charlotte. *Montages ins Blauen: Moholy-Nagy 1922–1943*. Berlin: Anabas, 1980.

Malhotra, Ruth, et al. *Das Frühe Plakat in Europa and den USA*. Berlin: Mann Verlag. Vol. 1 (*British and American Posters*), 1973; vol. 2 (*French and Belgian Posters*), 1977; vol. 3 (*German Posters*), 1980.

Margadant, Bruno: *The Swiss Poster, 1900–1983*. Basel: Birkhaus, 1983.

Mazzocchi, Gianni, and Renzo Trionfera. *Paolo Garretto Story*. Milan: Domus, 1983.

McClinton, Katharine Morrison. *Art Deco: A Guide for Collectors*. New York: Clarkson N. Potter, 1972.

McKnight-Kauffer, E. *The Art of the Poster*. London: Cecil Palmer, 1924.

McLean, Ruari. *Jan Tschichold: Typographer*. Boston: David R. Godine, 1975.

Meggs, Philip B. *A History of Graphic Design*. New York: Van Nostrand Reinhold Co., 1983.

Menten, Theodore. *Advertising Art in the Art Deco Style*. New York: Dover Publications, 1975.

Meyer, Susan E. *America's Great Illustrators*. New York: Harry N. Abrams, 1978.

Mott, Frank Luther. *A History of American Magazines*. Vol. 3. Cambridge: Harvard University Press, 1957.

———. *A History of American Magazines*. Vol. 5. Cambridge: Harvard University Press, 1968.

Mouron, Henri. *A. M. Cassandre*. New York: Rizzoli, 1985.

Müller-Brockmann, Josef, and Shizuko. *History of the Poster*. Zurich: ABC Verlag, 1971.

Naylor, Gillian. *The Bauhaus*. London: Studio Vista, 1968.

Neumann, Eckhard. *Functional Graphic Design in the 20s*. New York: Reinhold, 1967.

Pabst, Michael. *Wiener Grafik um 1900*. Munich: Verlag Silke Schreiber, 1984.

Packer, William. *The Art of Vogue Covers: 1909–1940*. New York: Harmony Books, 1980.

Pichon, Léon. *The New Book Illustration in France*. London: Studio, Ltd., 1924.

Pitz, Henry C. *Two Hundred Years of American Illustration*. New York: Random House, 1977.

Poiret, Paul. *The King of Fashion*. Philadelphia: J. B. Lippincott, 1933.

Price, Charles Matlack. *Poster Design*. New York: George W. Bricka, 1913.

Rademacher, Helmut. *Das Deutsche Plakat: Von den Anfängen bis zur Gegenwart*. Dresden: VEB Verlag der Kunst, 1965.

———. *Masters of German Poster Art*. Leipzig: Edition Leipzig, 1966.

Rickards, Maurice. *Posters of the Twenties*. London: Evelyn, Adams and Mackay, 1968.

Ridley, Pauline. *Fashion Illustration*. New York: Rizzoli, 1979.

Robinson, Julian. *The Golden Age of Style*. London: Orbis Publishing, 1976.

Rosenberg, Harold. *Discovering the Present: Three Decades in Art, Culture, and Politics*. Chicago: University of Chicago Press, 1973.

Rosenblum, Robert. *Cubism and Twentieth-Century Art*. London: Thames and Hudson, 1961. New York: Harry N. Abrams, 1961.

Rubin, William S. *Dada and Surrealist Art*. New York: Harry N. Abrams, 1968. London: Thames and Hudson, 1969.

———, ed. *Pablo Picasso: A Retrospective*. New York: Museum of Modern Art, 1980.

Schnessel, S. Michael. *Icart*. New York: Clarkson N. Potter, 1976.

Shackleton, J. T. *The Golden Age of the Railway Poster*. Paris: New English Library, 1976.

Spencer, Charles. *Erté*. New York: Clarkson N. Potter, 1970.

———. *The World of Serge Diaghilev*. Chicago: Henry Regnery Co., 1974.

Spencer, Herbert. *Pioneers of Modern Typography*. London: Lund Humphries Publishers, 1969.

Swanberg, W. A. *Luce and His Empire*. New York: Charles Scribner's Sons, 1972.

Torrens, Deborah. *Fashion Illustrated: A Review of Woman's Dress, 1920–1950*. New York: Hawthorn Books, 1975.

Tschichold, Jan. *Leben und Werk des Typographen*. Dresden: VEB Verlag der Kunst, 1977.

Vergo, Peter. *Art in Vienna, 1898–1918*. London: Phaidon Press, 1975.

Verneuil, M. P. *Eric deCoulon*. Neuchâtel, Switzerland: Éditions de la Baconnière, 1933.

Vienot, Jacques. *Cappiello*. Paris: Éditions de Clemont, 1964.

Waissenberger, Robert. *Vienna Secession*. New York: Rizzoli, 1971.

Watrous, James. *A Century of American Printmaking, 1880–1980*. London: University of Wisconsin Press, 1984.

Weill, Alain. *L'Affiche dans le Monde*. Paris: Éditions Aimery Somogy, 1984. Boston: G. K. Hall and Co., 1985.

———. *100 Years of Posters of the Folies Bergère and Music Halls of Paris*. New York: Images Graphiques, 1977.

Weitenkampf, Frank. *The Illustrated Book*. Cambridge, Mass.: Harvard University Press, 1938.

Willett, John. *The New Sobriety, 1917–1933: Art and Politics in the Weimar Period*. London: Thames and Hudson, 1978.

Wiser, William. *The Crazy Years: Paris in the Twenties*. New York: Atheneum Publishers, 1983.

Witkin, Lee D., and Barbara London. *The Photograph Collector's Guide*. Boston: New York Graphic Society, 1979.

EXHIBITION AND AUCTION CATALOGUES

L'Affiche en Belgique 1880–1980. Paris: Musée de l'Affiche, 1980.

Album de l'Exposition Internationale des Arts Décoratifs. Edité par l'Art Vivant. Paris: Libraire Larousse, 1925.

Les Années '25: Art Deco/Bauhaus/Stijl/Esprit Nouveau. Paris: Musée des Arts Décoratifs, 1966.

Art Deco. New York: Finch College Museum of Art, 1970.

Art Deco 1920–1930. Milan: Galleria Milano, 1965.

Le Arti A Vienna. Milan: Mazzotta Editore Edizioni La Biennale, 1984.

L'Avant Gard en Hongrie 1910–1930. Quimper: Galerie Arts et Civilisations, 1984.

Brave New Worlds—America's Futurist Vision. Miami: Mitchell Wolfson Jr. New World Center Campus, Miami-Dade Community College, 1984.

Buildings: Architecture in American Modernism. New York: Hirschl and Adler Galleries, 1980.

Jean Carlu. Paris: Musée de l'Affiche, 1980.

A Century of Posters 1870–1970 by Jack Rennert. New York: Phillips, 1979.

Cinquantenaire de L'Exposition de 1925. Paris: Musée des Arts Décoratifs, 1976.

Contrasts of Form: Geometric Abstract Art 1910–1980. New York: Museum of Modern Art, 1985.

Constructivism and Futurism: Russian and Others. New York: Ex Libris, 1977.

The Cubist Print. Washington D.C.: National Gallery of Art, 1982.

Dada and Duchamp. New York: Ex Libris, 1974–75.

The Engraved Work of Eric Gill. London: Victoria and Albert Museum, 1977.

Exposition A. M. Cassandre. Paris: Musée des Arts Décoratifs, 1950.

Exposition Coloniale Internationale de Paris. Paris: Musée des Colonies, 1931.

Fashion 1900–1939. London: Victoria and Albert Museum, n.d.

Paolo Garretto. Milan: Square Gallery, 1973.

Ludwig Hohlwein—Plakat der Jahre 1906–1940. Stuttgart: Staatsgalerie, 1985.

Internationale Plakate 1871–1971. Munich: Haus der Kunst, 1971.

Paul Iribe, Précurseur de l'Art Deco. Hôtel de Sens. Paris: Bibliothèque Forney, 1983.

Italy 1900–1945. Miami: Mitchell Wolfson Jr. New World Center Campus, Miami-Dade Community College, 1985.

Béla Kádár, A Leading Expressionist in the Twenties of "Der Sturm" in Berlin. New York: Paul Kövesdy Gallery, 1985.

Lajos Kassák Retrospective Exhibition. New York: Matignon Gallery, 1984.

Lambert-Rucki. Berlin: Sammlung Bröhan, 1979.

Fernand Léger. Buffalo: Albright-Knox Art Gallery, 1982.

Tamara de Lempicka. Paris: Galerie du Luxembourg, 1972.

Georges Lepape 1887–1971. Paris: Galerie du Luxembourg, 1978.

Livres Illustrés 1900–1930. Geneva: Slatkine Beaux Livres, c. 1984.

Charles Loupot. Paris: Musée de l'Affiche, n.d.

Major Art Movements of Twentieth Century Art II. New York: Ex Libris, 1976.

Major Art Movements of Twentieth Century Art III. New York: Ex Libris, 1978.

100 Poster Masterpieces by Jack Rennert. New York: Phillips, 1981.

Painting in France 1900–1967, circulated by the International Exhibitions Foundation. Washington, D.C.: National Portrait Gallery of Art, 1968.

Paris—Moscou. Musée National d'Art Moderne. Paris: Centre Georges Pompidou, 1980.

Paris—New York. Musée National d'Art Moderne. Paris: Centre Georges Pompidou, 1980.

Plakate. Munich: Galerie Ilse Schwein Steiger, 1985.

Plakate in München 1840–1940. Munich: Münchner Stadtmuseum, 1975.

The Poster (1865–1969). Nihonbashi and Nanba, Japan: Takashimaya Art Galleries, 1985.

Posters by A. M. Cassandre. New York: Museum of Modern Art, 1936.

Premier Posters by Jack Rennert. New York: Poster Auctions International, 1985.

The School of Paris. New York: Museum of Modern Art, 1965.

De Stijl: 1917–1931, Visions of Utopia. Minneapolis: Walker Art Center, 1982.

Timeless Images. Tokyo: Isetan Museum of Art, 1984.

Wendingen 1918–1931. Florence: Palazzo Medici-Ricardi, 1982.

The World of Art Deco. Minneapolis: Minneapolis Institute of Arts, 1971.

PERIODICALS

Art & Industry. London and New York: Studio, Ltd., 1922–39. (Some issues also known as *Commercial Art and Industry*.)

Arts et Métiers Graphiques. Paris, 1927–39.

Art Deco Society News. New York. Vol. 3, no. 4 (winter 1983); vol. 4, no. 2 (summer 1984).

Gebrausgraphik-International Advertising Art. Berlin: Phonix Illustrationsdruck und Verlag, 1925–44.

Modern Publicity—Commercial Art Annual, F. A. Mercer and W. Gaunt, eds. London: Studio, Ltd., 19 –3.

Das Plakat, Hans Sachs, ed. Berlin: Vereins der Plakatfreunde, 1909–21. (From 1909 to 1912 known as *Vereins der Plakatfreunde*.)

The Poster. Chicago: Poster Advertising Assoc., 1915–38.

Posters & Publicity—Fine Printing & Design, Geoffrey Holmes, ed. London: Studio, Ltd., 1927–39.

Die Reklame. Berlin: Verband Deutscher Reklamefachleute, 1907–32.

Wendingen. Amsterdam: H. Th. Wydeveld, 1918–31.

Notes

1. Herbert Bayer, *Herbert Bayer painter designer architect* (New York: Reinhold, 1967).

2. Ibid.

3. From an interview in *Idler*, quoted by Bevis Hillier, *Posters* (New York: Stein and Day, 1967).

4. E. McKnight-Kauffer, *The Art of the Poster* (London: Cecil Palmer, 1924).

5. Jan Tschichold, *El Lissitzky 1890–1941* (Sophie Lissitzky-Küppers, 1965).

6. *Jean Carlu,* exhibition catalogue (Paris: Musée de l'Affiche, 1980).

7. The original spelling was *Bazar*. The third "a" was added in November 1929.

A NOTE ON THE TYPE

The typeface used for the text of this book is Bodoni, one of the many
similar faces named after the great eighteenth-century Italian printer
Giambattista Bodoni and popular in the Art Deco era. The chapter titles
are set in Gill Sans Ultrabold, a variation of the seminal sans-serif alphabet
designed by Eric Gill in 1928. Premier Liteline is the face used for the
headings of the illustration subsections. It is very characteristic of letter
designs used by Deco artists to express elegance—a major concern
of the period.